Algebra

Credits

Author: Theresa Kane McKell

Production: Quack & Company, Inc.

Illustrations: Jeff VanKanegan

Cover Design: Matthew VanZomeren

This book has been correlated to state, national, and Canadian provincial standards. Visit *www.carsondellosa.com* to search for and view its correlations to your standards.

Introduction

Algebra provides students with the conceptual information needed to solve most algebraic problems. It also can be used as a tool in creating a deeper understanding of the necessary skills required to solve these problems. This book includes a variety of drill and practice problems along with an overview of each skill to be practiced. It is designed to meet the needs of any student at any level of algebra.

The main objective of this book is to give students the opportunity to find success in algebra. To aid in this experience, the book offers an explanation of each individual skill followed by a variety of activities. These activities will ensure the complete understanding of each skill introduced. Included on page 3 is an "Algebra Topics and Notes Sheet." This sheet provides students with a place to write facts, figures, and examples for each topic covered. A grid sheet is provided on page 4 which can be copied to complete algebraic graphs.

Algebra is divided into 12 sections. Each section contains a set of drill and practice student pages, a review of these pages, and a test of the skills learned throughout the section. Each student page consists of a description of the particular skill, several examples, and problems for the students to work to practice learning the skill. Along with the skills the students will learn, they will also get the chance to discover the relationship of algebraic skills to the real world through writing and problem solving.

The concepts covered in this book are relative to most any Algebra I course. The students will develop a conceptual understanding of the algebraic topics and will practice the skills relating to algebraic concepts. Some of the concepts include algebraic expressions and equations; order of operations; the writing, solving, graphing, and applying of linear equations; and the calculation of inequalities and absolute values.

Algebra is a great way to challenge students and to aid those in need of extra practice. Either focus for this book will yield the same result—an increased interest and understanding of valuable algebraic concepts. Observe as your students experience how stimulating algebra can be.

Table of Contents

Algebra Topics and Notes Sheet

Topic: _____

Notes:

Examples:

Name _____   Date _____

Graphs for _____
(title of worksheet)

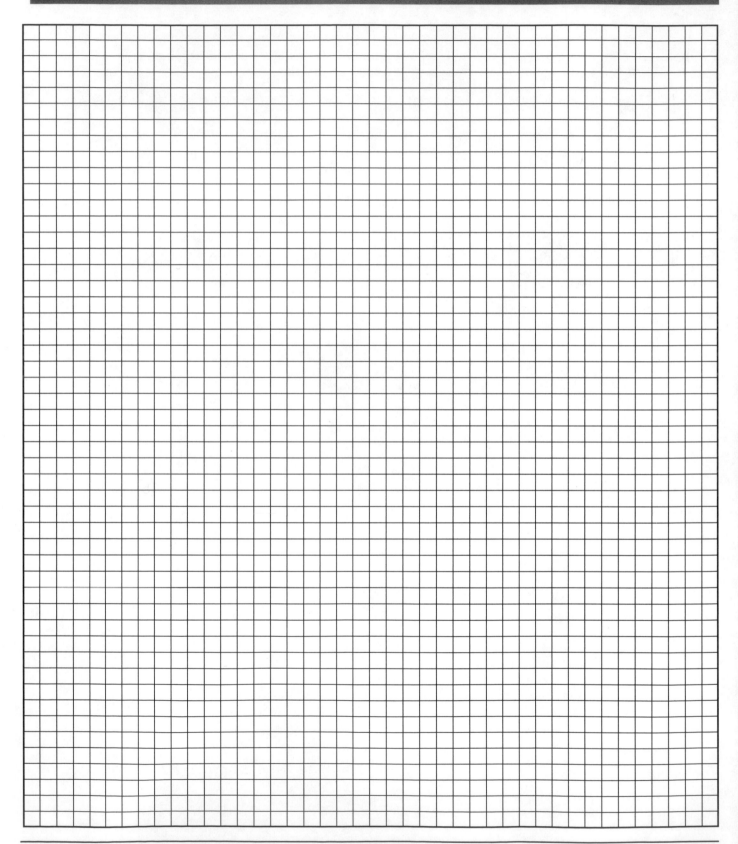

Algebraic expressions

Connecting with Algebra

A mathematical expression is a grouping of numbers that contains no equal sign. A numerical expression contains one or more numbers and/or one or more operations.

| 14 | 5 + 4 | 8.9 | 13 − 6 + 10 | 12 ÷ 3 • 5 |

A variable is a symbol (usually a letter) that represents one or more numbers. An algebraic expression contains one or more variables and can also contain one or more operations.

$2n$ (meaning $2 \times n$) $\frac{x}{y}$ (meaning x divided by y) $s + 7 - t$

To evaluate an algebraic expression, replace each variable with a number and find its numerical value.

$7n$, $n = 4$ (4 is the value given for n) $5rs$, $r = 2$, $s = 10$ $\frac{t}{e}$, $t = 4$, $e = 2$

$7 \cdot n = 7 \cdot 4$ (substitute 4 for n) $5 \cdot r \cdot s = 5 \cdot 2 \cdot 10$ $\frac{t}{e} = 4 \div 2$

= 28 (the result)   = 100   = 2

Circle each problem that is an expression. Write an **X** if it is not an expression.

1. $5 + 4 - 2 = 7$ **2.** $10 \div 5 - 3$ **3.** $12 - 4 \div 2 = 10$ **4.** $8 \cdot 4 = 32$

5. $4 + r$ **6.** $7 + t = 18$ **7.** $6mn$ **8.** $9 - 3 + 5$

Evaluate each expression.

9. $6 + 10 - 5$ **10.** $\frac{a}{b}$, $a = 45$, $b = 15$ **11.** $\frac{u}{4}$, $u = 20$

12. $8w$, $w = 3$ **13.** $24 - t$, $t = 9$ **14.** $10 + 5 + 15 - 9$

15. $e - f$, $e = 20$, $f = 7$ **16.** $x + y$, $x = 21$, $y = 13$ **17.** jkh, $j = 2$, $k = 6$, $h = 7$

Write an algebraic expression for each description below.

18. 9 more than r **19.** the cost of b tickets at $20 a ticket

20. twice the number t **21.** $\frac{2}{3}$ the length c of a bus

22. 9 subtracted from y **23.** three times the number x divided by 10

Order of operations

To simplify an expression, use the order of operations to calculate the answer. The order of operations is as follows:

1. parentheses ( ) and brackets [ ], called grouping symbols (worked from the inside out)
2. exponents
3. multiplication and division (worked from left to right)
4. addition and subtraction (worked from left to right)

$5 + 12 \div 4$	$6[10 - (2 + 8)]$	$9 - 3y,\ y = 2$	$7a - 9b,\ a = 3,\ b = 2$
$5 + 3$	$6[10 - 10]$	$9 - 3 \cdot 2$	$7 \cdot 3 - 9 \cdot 2$
8	$6 \cdot 0$	$9 - 6$	$21 - 18$
	0	3	3

State the first operation to be performed in each expression.

1. $4 \cdot 7 - 5$

2. $(10 + 4) - 2 \cdot 5$

3. $7 - 2 + 5 - 1$

4. $8 - 18 \div 6$

5. $9 + 8 \div 2$

6. $18 \div 9 + 3$

7. $9 \cdot 6 \div 9$

8. $2(4(12 - 7) + 5)$

Simplify.

9. $14 + 7 \cdot 3$

10. $2(5 - (3 + 1) + 13)$

11. $33 - 4(15 \div 3)$

12. $10 \div 2 - 3$

13. $24 - (18 + 4 - 10 \cdot 2)$

14. $19 + 3((8 + 3) - 9 \div 3)$

Evaluate.

15. $14 \cdot 4 \div r,\ r = 2$

16. $7a - 3 \cdot 5,\ a = 5$

17. $22 - 22 \div s,\ s = 2$

18. $18 - 3x,\ x = 4$

19. $16 + y \div 8,\ y = 48$

20. $12x + 7,\ x = 5$

Exponents and powers

Connecting with Algebra

Exponents are used to represent repeated multiplication. An exponent represents the number of times the base is used as a factor. For example, 3^4 is an expression used to represent 3 that is a factor 4 times. The number 3 is the base, the number 4 is the exponent, and 3^4 is the power.

$2 \bullet 2 \bullet 2 \bullet 2 \bullet 2 = 2^5$ Evaluate x^3 when $x = 4$ $(2x)^2$, $x = 3$

$3 \bullet 3 \bullet 5 \bullet 5 \bullet 5 \bullet 5 = 3^2 5^4$ $x^3 = 4 \bullet 4 \bullet 4$ $(2x)^2 = (2 \bullet 3)^2$

$\qquad\qquad\qquad\qquad\qquad\qquad\quad = 64$ $\qquad = 36$

It is important to remember the order of operations when evaluating expressions that involve exponents. Remember: parentheses, exponents, multiplication/division, and addition/subtraction.

Write each expression in exponent form.

1. $3 \bullet 3 \bullet 3 \bullet 3 \bullet 3 \bullet 3$

2. $a \bullet a \bullet b \bullet b \bullet b$

3. $9 \bullet 9$

4. $x \bullet x \bullet x \bullet y$

5. $10 \bullet 10 \bullet 10 \bullet 10 \bullet 10$

6. $4 \bullet 4 \bullet 4 \bullet 4 \bullet 4 \bullet 5 \bullet 5 \bullet 5 \bullet 5$

Simplify.

7. 2^3

8. $(35 - 5)^2 + 15$

9. 6^2

10. $35 - 5^2$

11. $7^2 \bullet 2$

12. $6^2 - 3 \bullet 5$

13. $5^3 \bullet 3$

14. $(8 + 2)^3$

Evaluate.

15. $4x^2 + 2x$, $x = 4$

16. $6r^2 + r$, $r = 5$

17. $k^2 - 2k + 12$, $k = 4$

18. $t^2 + 3t - 4$, $t = 3$

19. $(2y)^3 + 2y$, $y = 5$

20. $24 - 10s + 6s^2$, $s = 2$

Name   Date

Geometric formulas   **Connecting with Algebra**

Just as variables are used in algebra, they are also used in geometric situations. Geometric formulas often use letters to represent the sides of geometric shapes. The **perimeter** of a figure is the total distance around. The **area** of a figure is the number of square units it contains. The perimeter and area of geometric figures can be represented with formulas.

   Perimeter of a square = $4s$, where s is the length of one side
   Perimeter of a rectangle = $2\ell + 2w$, where ℓ is the length and w is the width
   Area of a square = s^2, where s is the length of one side
   Area of a rectangle = ℓw, where ℓ is the length and w is the width
   Area of a triangle = $\frac{1}{2}bh$, where b is the base and h is the height

Look at these examples.

The area of a square with a side length of 4 inches:
   $a = s^2 = 4^2 = 4 \cdot 4 = 16$ in.^{2}

The perimeter of a rectangle with a length of 10 cm and a width of 3 cm:
   $P = 2\ell + 2w = 2 \cdot 10 + 2 \cdot 3 = 20 + 6 = 26$ cm

Use $P = 4s$ to find the perimeter of each square.

1. $s = 12$ ft.   **2.** $s = 20$ cm

3. $s = 7$ in.   **4.** $s = 18$ mm

Use $P = 2\ell + 2w$ to find the perimeter of each rectangle.

5. $\ell = 13$ in., $w = 5$ in.

6. $\ell = 2$ cm, $w = 20$ cm

First identify the formula to use from the letters given, then use that formula to find the area of the figure given its dimensions.

7. $b = 7$ in., $h = 4$ in.   **8.** $s = 13$ mm   **9.** $\ell = 2.1$ yd., $w = 7$ yd.

10. $s = 6$ cm   **11.** $b = 20$ ft., $h = 5$ ft.   **12.** $s = 3.4$ in.

13. $\ell = 15$ ft., $w = 3$ ft.   **14.** $\ell = 24$ cm, $w = 8$ cm   **15.** $b = 30$ mm, $h = 2$ mm

Commutative and associative properties   **Connecting with Algebra**

The commutative property of addition: For all numbers a and b, $a + b = b + a$.

The commutative property of multiplication: For all numbers a and b, $a \cdot b = b \cdot a$.

$$8 + 10 = 10 + 8 \qquad\qquad 8 \cdot 10 = 10 \cdot 8$$
$$x + y = y + x \qquad\qquad x \cdot y = y \cdot x$$
$$\frac{1}{2} + \frac{3}{4} = \frac{3}{4} + \frac{1}{2} \qquad\qquad \frac{1}{2} \cdot \frac{3}{4} = \frac{3}{4} \cdot \frac{1}{2}$$

The associative property of addition: For all numbers a, b, and c, $(a + b) + c = a + (b + c)$.

The associative property of multiplication: For all numbers a, b, and c, $(a \cdot b) \cdot c = a \cdot (b \cdot c)$.

$$(2 + 4) + 6 = 2 + (4 + 6)$$
$$(2 \cdot 4) \cdot 6 = 2 \cdot (4 \cdot 6)$$
$$(s + t) + u = s + (t + u)$$
$$(s \cdot t) \cdot u = s \cdot (t \cdot u)$$

Label each of the following with the appropriate property: **associative property of addition, associative property of multiplication, commutative property of addition,** or **commutative property of multiplication**.

1. $c + d = d + c$

2. $(x \cdot 4) \cdot 2 = x \cdot (4 \cdot 2)$

3. $(1 + 2) + 3 = 1 + (2 + 3)$

4. $17 + 14 = 14 + 17$

5. $12.1 \cdot 3 = 3 \cdot 12.1$

6. $32 \cdot 24 = 24 \cdot 32$

Circle each expression that is equivalent.

7. $(4 + 6) \cdot 2 = (4 + 6) \div 2$

8. $2 \cdot (33 \cdot t) = (2 \cdot 33) \cdot t$

9. $5 + (b + 3) = (b + 3) + 5$

10. $(\frac{1}{4} \cdot 4)x = x + (\frac{1}{4} \cdot 4)$

Simplify.

11. $4(3a)$ **12.** $8(7n)$ **13.** $4t(4)5$ **14.** $3r(4)2$

15. $(5x)2$ **16.** $3(6k)5$ **17.** $(tx)y$ **18.** $(ef)(gh)$

Distributive property   **Connecting with Algebra**

The distributive property: For all numbers a, b, and c,
$$a(b + c) = ab + ac \quad \text{and}$$
$$(b + c)a = ba + ca.$$

To distribute means to give something to each group. In the example, a is distributed to each letter, b and c.

$4(2 + 7) = 4 \cdot 2 + 4 \cdot 7$ $(10 - 8)3 = 10 \cdot 3 - 8 \cdot 3$ $3(2a + 4b - 6) = 3 \cdot 2a + 3 \cdot 4b - 3 \cdot 6$
$\quad\quad\quad = 8 + 28$ $\quad\quad\quad\quad = 30 - 24$ $\quad\quad\quad\quad\quad = 6a + 12b - 18$
$\quad\quad\quad = 36$ $\quad\quad\quad\quad = 6$

Rewrite using the distributive property.

1. $4 \cdot 8 + 4 \cdot 9 + 4 \cdot 2$ **2.** $6 \cdot 7 + 5 \cdot 7 - 9 \cdot 7$ **3.** $8 \cdot a - 5 \cdot a$

4. $8 \cdot 3 - 8 \cdot 7$ **5.** $x \cdot 3 + x \cdot 4 + x \cdot 10$ **6.** $kt + kr + ks$

Rewrite using the distributive property and then simplify.

7. $9(8 + 7)$ **8.** $10(7 - 3)$ **9.** $(2x - 3y)6$ **10.** $5(6y - 12)$

11. $(12 - 5)3$ **12.** $(10 + 12 + 14)2$ **13.** $10(x - y - z)$ **14.** $(x - 2z)7$

Simplify.

15. $4(3a + 5b + 6c + 8d + 2e + f)$ **16.** $(12w - 2x - 9y + 6z)10$

17. Show that $5(3y - 2) = 15y - 10$ for at least 5 values of y.

18. Show that $3(8x - 7) = 24x - 21$ for at least 5 values of x.

Combination of like terms

The expression $3x^2 + 2x + 1$ has three terms, $3x^2$, $2x$, and 1. The definition of terms in an expression is those parts of the expression connected by addition. A term in an expression without a variable is called a constant, as 1 is above. For terms to be considered "like" terms, they must have the same variable and corresponding variables must have the same exponents. All constant terms are considered "like" terms.

like terms	unlike terms
$3x$ and $8x$	$9y$ and $10z$
$2x^2y$ and $3x^2y$	$3ab$ and $4ac$

In the example, $3x$ and $8x$ are like terms with numerical coefficients of 3 and 8. A numerical coefficient of a term is simply the number before its corresponding variable. When combining like terms, simply keep the variable the same and combine the numerical coefficients.

$$4y + 10y = 14y \qquad 6b + 9b - 5b = 10b$$

$$10x - 3x = 8x \qquad 12x^2y - 10x^2y + 2x^2y = 4x^2y$$

Identify the like terms in each problem.

1. $7c + 12c - 2$ **2.** $19y - 10$ **3.** $12rt - 10r + 18t$

4. $5r - 10r + 8rs$ **5.** $5t + 7t - 1$ **6.** $q + 9 + 2q + 5q$

Simplify. If not possible, write **already simplified**.

7. $8m - 3m$ **8.** $8y + 12y + 3y$ **9.** $3s + 4(7s - 2)$

10. $2 + 10k$ **11.** $8q + 10q + 14$ **12.** $4 + 8x + 11y$

13. $5a + 6a - 9a$ **14.** $t + 8m + 4t - 4m$ **15.** $4(5w + 2) + w$

Simplify. Then evaluate given the value of the variable.

16. $6(3a + 4) + 5(4a - 2)$, $a = 5$ **17.** $5(b + 7) + 2b - 14 + (b + 10)$, $b = 8$

Name _____   Date _____

Equations and inequalities are considered mathematical sentences. An equation is simply two expressions connected together by an equal sign. An inequality is two expressions with an inequality symbol, such as $>$, $<$, or $\neq$ between them. Mathematical sentences can be either true or false.

$$9(5 - 4) = 10$$ $$27 - (5 + 20) = 2$$
$$9(1) = 9 \neq 10, \text{ so false}$$ $$27 - 25 = 2 = 2, \text{ so true}$$

Mathematical sentences can also be called open sentences. This is when the equation or inequality has a variable, such as $3x + 4 = 10$ or $2x - 10 > 15$. An open sentence is neither true nor false until the variable is replaced with numbers that make the sentence true. These numbers that can replace the variable are called the replacement set of numbers for the variable. The solution set of numbers for an open sentence is simply the numbers that are part of the replacement set that make the sentence true.

For example, with a replacement set of {2, 4, 6}, $3x + 4 = 10$ has a solution set of {2} because $3 \cdot 2 + 4 = 10$ is a true sentence. With the replacement set of {10, 12, 14}, the inequality $2x - 10 > 15$ has a solution set of {14} because $2 \cdot 14 - 10 > 15$ is a true sentence. If no number in the replacement set makes the sentence true, then the solution set of the sentence is simply the empty set, or the null set, written $\emptyset$.

Write **true** or **false**.

1. $7 > 4$

2. $9 + 11 < 21$

3. $8 > 4 + 5$

4. $2(6 + 8) \neq 3 \cdot 9$

Write **yes** or **no** to tell whether each number is in the solution set for the open sentence.

5. $14 = x + 2$; 12

6. $6.7 \neq b$; 6.7

7. $2x - 10 < 14$; 10

8. $14 - x \geq 7$; 7

9. $15 - y > 9$; 6

10. $x + 15 = 20$; 5

11. $a^2 > a$; 2

12. $4c - 4 < 15$; 5

Find the solution set for each problem if the replacement set is {0, 1, 2, 3, 4}.

13. $5x - 10 < 8$

14. $3x + 6 = 4x + 4$

15. $4x + 10 \neq x + 9$

Find the solution set for each problem if the replacement set is {2, 4, 6, 8}.

16. $7x - 2 = 8x - 8$

17. $2y + 3 \leq 3y + 2$

18. $5z + 10 > 4z + 12$

Name _____   Date _____

Review of Unit 1

Topics covered:
       Algebraic Expressions   Commutative and Associative Properties
       Order of Operations   Distributive Property
       Exponents and Powers   Combination of Like Terms
       Geometric Formulas   Solution Sets of Sentences

List the order of operations.

1. _____   **2.** _____

3. _____   **4.** _____

Write whether each is an **expression, equation,** or an **inequality**.

5. $3 + 5 - 7 = 1$ **6.** $3x - 5t + 4$ **7.** $9r + 10 \geq 14$ **8.** $10 + s \neq 4$

Evaluate.

9. $A = \frac{1}{2}bh$, $b = 10m$ and $h = 6m$ **10.** $A = s^2$, $s = 12$ in.

11. $x((4 + 5) - 8)$, $x = 2$ **12.** a^3b^2, $a = 3$, $b = 2$

13. $5x^2 + 8 - 15$, $x = 3$ **14.** $P = 2\ell + 2w$, $\ell = 5$ in. and $w = 8$ in.

Write whether each is an example of **commutative, associative,** or **distributive** properties.

15. $(c + g) \cdot f = f \cdot (c + g)$ **16.** $3(a + b) = 3a + 3b$ **17.** $(t - v)w = tw - vw$

18. $17 + 4 = 4 + 17$ **19.** $(x + y) + z = x + (y + z)$ **20.** $(10 \cdot 5) \cdot 2 = 10 \cdot (5 \cdot 2)$

Simplify.

21. $5t(2)(3)$ **22.** $7(a - b + 5)$ **23.** $9y + 15y - 10y$

24. $9(8n)$ **25.** $3k + 6k - 12$ **26.** $2t + 5m + 7t - 4m$

Find the solution set for each problem if the replacement set is {0, 1, 3, 5}.

27. $5x - 3 \geq 4x + 2$ **28.** $7x + 10 \neq 45$

Unit 1 Test

Write an algebraic expression for each description.

1. y subtracted from 10   **2.** 3 multiplied by s **3.** 11 more than r

Use the order of operations to simplify each expression.

4. $5 + t - 4 + 10$ **5.** $((9 - 7)^3 + 7) \div 5$ **6.** $3^3 \div 9 + 2$

7. $4 + 2(3^2 + 3 - 11)$ **8.** $3x + 5y - x + 6y$ **9.** $12 \times 2 \div 3 + 6$

Use the order of operations to evaluate each expression.

10. $4m + 7n,\ m = 4,\ n = 2$ **11.** $(18 + 3) \div b \cdot 5,\ b = 7$

12. $a^2 + a - 1,\ a = 3$ **13.** $A = \frac{1}{2}bh,\ b = 7m,\ h = 8\,m$

14. $(6 - 3)^2 + y^3,\ y = 2$ **15.** $P = 4s,\ s = 11$ in.

Give an example for each property: commutative property of addition (16), commutative property of multiplication (17), associative property of addition (18), associative property of multiplication (19), and the distributive property (20 and 21).

16. _____   **17.** _____

18. _____   **19.** _____

20. _____   **21.** _____

Find the solution set for each problem if the replacement set is {0, 5, 10}.

22. $2x + 7 \le 5x - 10$ **23.** $3x \ne 4x + 10$ **24.** $7x - 3 \ge 6x + 2$

Name _____   Date _____

The real number line

Real numbers are all of the numbers that are used in algebra. These numbers can be pictured as points on a horizontal line called a real number line. A starting point for all number lines is the origin, which is the point 0. The numbers to the left of 0 are the negative numbers. The numbers to the right of 0 are the positive numbers. Zero is neither positive nor negative. Below is an example of a number line with -4 and -2 as the negative numbers and 3 and 5 as the positive numbers.

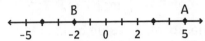

When graphing numbers on a line, the point is called the graph of the number, and the number that corresponds to the point is called the coordinate of the point.

$$
\begin{array}{ccccc}
& B & & & A \\
-5 & -2 & 0 & 2 & 5
\end{array}
$$

In the above graph, point A is the graph of the number 5. The number 5 is the coordinate of point A. Point B is the graph of the number -2. The number -2 is the coordinate of the point B.

Give the coordinate of each point graphed.

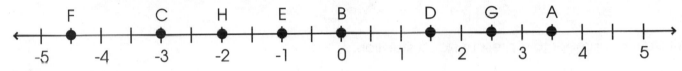

1. A   **2.** B   **3.** C   **4.** D   **5.** E   **6.** F   **7.** G   **8.** H

On the number line, graph each point whose coordinate is given.

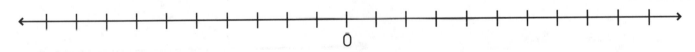

9. A: -2   **10.** B: $3\frac{1}{2}$ **11.** C: $-4\frac{1}{2}$ **12.** D: 0   **13.** E: $-1\frac{1}{2}$ **14.** F: 5

Write each set of numbers in increasing order.

15. 2.1, -1.8, 3, 0, $\frac{1}{3}$, $-\frac{1}{3}$ **16.** 7.5, $-\frac{1}{2}$, 7, -5.4, $\frac{3}{4}$, $\frac{1}{2}$

17. 18, -15, 12, 3, -13, -11   **18.** -6, -8, 13, 4, 5, -10

Use < or > to make each statement true.

19. 8 _____ 4   **20.** -3 _____ 1   **21.** $2\frac{1}{2}$ _____ 3   **22.** $-3\frac{1}{3}$ _____ 3

23. 0 _____ -4   **24.** $4\frac{1}{4}$ _____ 4   **25.** -9 _____ -6   **26.** 2 _____ -3

Opposites (additive inverses) and absolute value   **Using Rules of Algebra**

Every real number has an opposite. Opposite numbers are the same distance from 0 on a number line and lie on the opposite sides of 0. The opposite of a positive number is a negative number. The opposite of a negative number is a positive number. The numbers 3 and –3 are opposites. Find their graphs on the real number line to the right. The additive inverse of a number is the same as the opposite of a number. Remember, the opposite of 0 is simply 0 since it is neither positive nor negative.

The symbol $|x|$ is called the absolute value of x. The absolute value of a number is the distance between the number and 0 on a number line. The absolute value of a number, whether positive or negative, is always positive.

$$|10| = 10 \qquad |-2| = 2 \qquad |-102| = 102 \qquad -|12| = -12$$

note: The answer to $-|12|$ is –12 because the absolute value of 12 is 12 but then it is multiplied by a negative, which resulted in –12.

Write the opposite of each number.

1. 5   **2.** -2.6   **3.** $-\frac{3}{4}$ **4.** 0   **5.** -40   **6.** 2.8

Write a real number to represent each situation.

7. a gain of 12 yards

8. a temperature drop of 8°

9. a deposit of $89.26

10. a withdrawal of $75

Write the absolute value of each number.

11. $|10|$ **12.** $|23|$ **13.** $|0|$ **14.** $|-42|$

Compare the following numbers. Use **<, >,** or **=** to make each statement true.

15. $|3.5|$ _____ $|-3.5|$ **16.** $|-4.2|$ _____ $|3.1|$ **17.** $-|-4|$ _____ $-|4|$

Simplify.

18. $-|-15|$ **19.** $|-5| \cdot |-4|$ **20.** $-|4 \cdot 3|$

21. $-|30 \div 6|$ **22.** $|-8| + |8|$ **23.** $|7| - |-7|$

Addition of real numbers

Using Rules of Algebra

A number line is a great way to model the addition of real numbers.

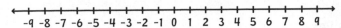

-9 -8 -7 -6 -5 -4 -3 -2 -1 0 1 2 3 4 5 6 7 8 9

Add 3 + 5. (Start at 3 and move 5 places to the right since 5 is positive.) The answer is 8.

Add 3 + (-5). (Start at 3 and move 5 places to the left since 5 is negative.) The answer is -2.

When adding a number that is positive, move to the right. When adding a number that is negative, move to the left.

Explain how to add the following numbers using a number line, and tell the result.

1. 7 + 8 _____

2. -5 + 9 _____

3. 10 + (-7) _____

4. -11 + (-6) _____

Use the number line to add the numbers.

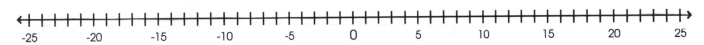

-25   -20   -15   -10   -5   0   5   10   15   20   25

5. 4 + 9

6. -5 + 13 + (-11)

7. -7 + (-6)

8. 14 + 10 + (-3)

9. 0 + (-5)

10. -6 + (-9) + 10

11. -3 + 3

12. 8 + (-2) + (-4) + 6

13. 7 + (-12)

14. -11 + 5 + (-13) + 8

15. -11 + 8 + (-1)

16. 12 + (-6) + (-14) + 17

Addition of real numbers

To add two real numbers with the same sign:

1. Add their absolute values.
2. Determine the sign of the answer.
   a. If both numbers are positive, then the answer is positive.
   b. If both numbers are negative, then the answer is negative.

$$-2 + (-3) = -5 \qquad 4 + 5 = 9 \qquad -10 + (-21) = -31$$

To add two real numbers with different signs, if the numbers are not opposites:

1. Subtract their absolute values, the larger number minus the smaller number.
2. The sign of the answer will be the same sign of the number with the larger absolute value.

$3 + (-10)$	$-12 + 4$	$-9 + 13$
$\lvert -10 \rvert - \lvert 3 \rvert$	$\lvert -12 \rvert - \lvert 4 \rvert$	$\lvert 13 \rvert - \lvert -9 \rvert$
$10 - 3 = 7$	$12 - 4 = 8$	$13 - 9 = 4$
answer: -7	answer: -8	answer: 4

Add.

1. $4 + 3$

2. $-12 + 4$

3. $19 + (-3) + 6$

4. $11 + 12$

5. $-21 + 0$

6. $-1 + (-4) + 18$

7. $-2 + 5$

8. $23 + (-15)$

9. $-7 + 8 + (-5)$

10. $7 + (-8)$

11. $-11 + 11$

12. $32 + (-15) + (-6)$

13. $-10 + (-15)$

14. $-22 + (-22)$

15. $13 + (-21) + 7$

Write an expression to represent each situation and solve.

16. A football team had a 5-yard loss followed by an 8-yard gain. Find the resulting gain or loss.

17. In one month, Jeff lost 8 pounds. The next month he gained 5 pounds. He lost 4 more pounds in the third month. Find the net gain or loss.

Name _____   Date _____

Subtraction of real numbers   **Using Rules of Algebra**

For all real numbers a and b, $a - b = a + (-b)$. Simply stated: To subtract a number, add its opposite.

$7 - 10 = 7 + (-10)$ $5 - 8 + 3 - 1 = 5 + (-8) + 3 + (-1)$ $-4 - (-12)$
$\quad\quad = -3$ $= 5 + 3 + (-8) + (-1)$ (group the + and $= -4 + 12$
                                 $= 8 + (-9)$ – numbers) $= 8$
                                 $= -1$

Change each problem into an addition problem.

1. $7 - 9$ **2.** $-6 - (-4)$

3. $-11 - 5$ **4.** $12 - (-15)$

5. $8 - 3$ **6.** $22 - 5$

7. $4 - 11$ **8.** $-4 - (-9)$

Subtract.

9. $9 - 11$ **10.** $0 - (-12)$

11. $-5 - 4$ **12.** $6 - (-6)$

13. $-1 - (-1)$ **14.** $-7 - 6$

15. $3 - (-5)$ **16.** $17 - 23$

Evaluate when $x = -2$, $y = -5$, and $z = 12$.

17. $x - y$ **18.** $y - x$ **19.** $x - z$ **20.** $z - y$

Multiplication of real numbers

The property of zero for multiplication: For all real numbers a, $a \cdot 0 = 0$ and $0 \cdot a = 0$.
Simply stated, any real number multiplied by 0 is 0. For example, $0 \cdot 20 = 0$ and $13 \cdot 0 = 0$
To multiply two real numbers with same signs:
   1. Multiply their absolute values.
   2. The sign of their product is positive.

positive • positive = positive   negative • negative = positive
   (+)   (+)   (+)   (-)   (-)   (+)
          $3 \cdot 12 = 36$ $-7 \cdot -8 = 56$

To multiply two real numbers with opposite signs:
   1. Multiply their absolute values.
   2. The sign of their product is negative.

negative • positive = negative   positive • negative = negative
   (−)   (+)   (-)   (+)   (−)   (−)
          $-2 \cdot 5 = -10$ $4 \cdot -8 = -32$

Write the sign of the product for each number.

1. $(-10)4$

2. $8(-1)$

3. $(-2)(-3)$

4. $(7)(5)(-3)$

5. $5(6)$

6. $(-2)(-7)$

7. $(-12)(-4)(-1)$

8. $(-6)(4)(-2)$

Multiply to find each product.

9. $4(6)(-1)$

10. $(-1)(-4)(-3)$

11. $(-\frac{1}{2})(2)$

12. $(7)(-3)(0)$

13. $(5)(3)$

14. $(-\frac{1}{8})(-16)(4)$

15. $(-9)(-4)$

16. $(-7)(7)$

A negative times a negative equals a positive!

Evaluate when $x = -3$, $y = -5$, and $z = 0$.

17. xy

18. $-3yz$

19. xy^2

20. $4x^2y^2z^2$

Division of real numbers

The multiplicative inverse property states that for each nonzero a, there is exactly one number $\frac{1}{a}$ such that: $a \cdot \frac{1}{a} = 1$ and $\frac{1}{a} \cdot a = 1$.

The number $\frac{1}{a}$ is called the reciprocal of a.

For example, the reciprocal of 9 is $\frac{1}{9}$ and the reciprocal of $\frac{1}{2}$ is 2. Simply flip the number to find its reciprocal.

To divide the number a by the number b, multiply a by the reciprocal of b.

$a \div b = a \cdot \frac{1}{b}$ (The result will be the quotient of a and b.)

Here are some examples.

$$12 \div 4 = 12 \cdot \frac{1}{4} \qquad 4x \div \frac{1}{4} = 4x \cdot 4 \qquad 15 \div \frac{3}{2} = 15 \cdot \frac{2}{3}$$
$$= 3 \qquad\qquad\qquad = 16x \qquad\qquad\qquad = 10$$

To divide two nonzero real numbers, remember:

1. The quotient is positive if both numbers have the same sign.
2. The quotient is negative if both numbers have different signs.

$$-15 \div 5 = -15 \cdot \frac{1}{5} \qquad 3 \div \frac{1}{4} = 3 \cdot 4 \qquad 1 \div -\frac{4}{5} = 1 \cdot -\frac{5}{4}$$
$$= -3 \qquad\qquad\qquad = 12 \qquad\qquad\qquad = -\frac{5}{4}$$

Write the reciprocal of each number. Write **none** if it does not exist.

1. 2

2. 1

3. 0

4. $-\frac{1}{9}$

5. $-\frac{1}{4}$

6. $\frac{4}{3}$

7. -8

8. 10

Divide.

9. $\frac{9}{3}$

10. $\frac{-28}{7}$

11. $-15 \div 0$

12. $\frac{-7}{8} \div \frac{1}{8}$

13. $\frac{36}{-4}$

14. $\frac{-8}{-8}$

15. $44 \div (-11)$

16. $0 \div \frac{4}{5}$

Simplify.

17. $-50 \div (40 \div (-20))$

18. $56 \div (-28 \div 7)$

19. $(-38 \div 19) \div (-2)$

20. $-45 \div (-20 \div (-4))$

Mixed operations

When simplifying problems using all the rules for operating with real numbers, be very careful not to confuse the rules.

$$-2 + (-8) = -10 \qquad -2 - (-8) = -2 + 8 \qquad -2 \cdot -8 = 16 \qquad -2 \div (-8) = -2 \cdot -\frac{1}{8}$$
$$= 6 \qquad\qquad\qquad\qquad\qquad\qquad\qquad = \frac{1}{4}$$

Remember:
1. The sum of two negative numbers is negative.
2. The difference between two negative numbers has the sign of the number with the greater absolute value.
3. The product of two negative numbers is positive.
4. The quotient of two negative numbers is positive.

Simplify.

1. $-3 + 4 \cdot -9$

2. $6 - 8^2$

3. $6^2 - (-1)^2$

4. $-4 \cdot 7 - 5$

5. $-2 + (-10)^2$

6. $11 - (-3)^3$

Evaluate each problem given each variable value.

7. $x^3 - 5$, $x = -4$

8. $-8 - 7t^2$, $t = -3$

9. $8 - 4y$, $y = 6$

10. $\frac{a + 6b}{-2a}$, $a = -2$, $b = 5$

Simplify. Then evaluate when $x = -2$, $y = -3$, and $z = 4$.

11. $3(4x + 2(8y - 7))$

12. $6x \div (2(6 + 4y)) - 3$

13. $-3x + 5(4z + 2(4 + 3y))$

14. $(2y - 3z) \div (-2x + 5)$

Like terms with real number coefficients

The property of -1 for multiplication states that for any real number a, $-1a = -a$ and $a(-1) = -a$.

$-a + 3a = (-1 + 3)a = 2a$ (The variable a has a coefficient -1. It is simply not written.)

$a + 3a = (1 + 3)a = 4a$ (The variable a has a coefficient 1. It is simply not written.)

To combine like terms with real number coefficients, use the rules of adding, subtracting, multiplying, and dividing real numbers and simplify.

$$-6ab - 7ab = (-6 - 7)ab$$
$$= [-6 + (-7)]ab$$
$$= -13ab$$

$$10y - 13 - 12y + 4 = (10 - 12)y + (-13 + 4)$$
$$= [10 + (-12)]y + (-9)$$
$$= -2y + (-9) = -2y - 9$$

Simplify.

1. $8y + 10y$

2. $-7b - 11b$

3. $-4r - t + 4r + 7t$

4. $-6x + 8x$

5. $-4c - c$

6. $-8d + 7w + (-8d) + 10w$

7. $3a - 5a$

8. $6s - 6s$

9. $-4a + 5b - a - 4b$

Write a formula for the perimeter of each rectangle. Simplify. Remember: The basic formula for the perimeter of a rectangle is $P = 2\ell + 2w$.

10.

```
        3x
┌──────────────┐
│              │  x + y
│              │
└──────────────┘
```

11.

```
      3y + 4x
┌──────────────┐
│              │  x - 2y
│              │
└──────────────┘
```

12.

```
     6x - y + 3
┌──────────────┐
│              │  5x + 3y - 4
│              │
└──────────────┘
```

negative factors

The distributive property states: $a(b + c) = ab + ac$, where a is multiplied by both b and c. When a is negative, a is a negative factor. Example, $-a(b + c) = -ab + (-ac)$, where the negative factor a is being distributed to both b and c making both products negative.

$$-3(2x + 9) = -3 \cdot 2x + (-3) \cdot 9$$
$$= -6x + -27$$
$$= -6x - 27$$

$$3x - (8 + 6x) = 3x - 1(8 + 6x)$$
$$= 3x + (-1)8 + (-1)6x$$
$$= 3x + -8 + (-6x)$$
$$= -3x - 8$$

Simplify.

1. $-8(3x + 2)$

2. $-6(4 + 2y) - 9$

3. $t - (7 - t)$

4. $-4(-8 + 4y)$

5. $3s - (4s + 5)$

6. $6 - (8 - b) - 4b$

7. $-(-a + b - 2)$

8. $10 - 8(5 - 6d) + 12d$

9. $-5(3z - 6) - 2(7 + 3z)$

Simplify. Then evaluate each problem given each variable value.

10. $-(-8x + 3) - 9x + 2$, $x = 4$

11. $-(6z - 9) - (10 - z)$, $z = -2$

12. $-9y - (6y + 5) + 11y$, $y = -1$

13. $7a - (9 - a) + 15$, $a = -5$

Rates and ratios

If a and b are two quantities measured in *different* units, then the average *rate* of a per b is $\frac{a}{b}$. For example, if a car was driven a distance of 200 miles and it used 10 gallons of gas, the average gas mileage would be:

$$\frac{200 \text{ miles}}{10 \text{ gallons}} = \frac{200}{10} \frac{\text{miles}}{\text{gallons}} = 20 \text{ miles per gallon}$$

If a and b are two quantities measured in the *same* units, then the *ratio* of a to b is $\frac{a}{b}$.

For example, if the baseball team won 12 out of its last 14 games, the win to loss ratio would be:

$$\text{win-loss ratio} = \frac{\text{games won}}{\text{games lost}} = \frac{12 \text{ games}}{2 \text{ games}} = \frac{12}{2}$$

Usually ratios are left in fraction form.

note: The difference between rates and ratios is that rates compare two quantities measured in different units and ratios compare two quantities measured in the same unit.

1. Explain the difference between a rate and a ratio.

Tell whether each of the following are describing a **rate** or a **ratio**. Write each unit in fraction form.

2. miles per hour

3. comparing areas of two rooms

4. hourly wage

5. comparing price of a single scoop of ice cream versus the whole container of ice cream

Solve.

6. A car uses 8 gallons of gas to travel 236 miles. Find the average number of miles per gallon.

7. You get paid $105 for working 20 hours. Find your hourly rate of pay.

8. You drove 245 miles in $3\frac{1}{2}$ hours. What was the average speed?

9. During a golf game, you scored an 84 on an 18-hole course. What was your average score per hole?

Name _____   Date _____

Topics covered:

The Real number Line	Division of Real numbers
Opposites (Additive Inverses) and Absolute Value	Mixed Operations
	Like Terms with Real number Coefficients
Addition of Real numbers	negative Factors
Subtraction of Real numbers	Rates and Ratios
Multiplication of Real numbers	

Graph each point on the number line.

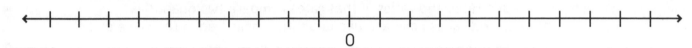

0

1. A: $-1\frac{1}{2}$ **2.** B: 2   **3.** C: -4   **4.** D: $3\frac{1}{2}$ **5.** E: 0

Write a real number to represent each situation. Then give its opposite.

6. a withdrawal of $12.96   **7.** a gain of 13 yards   **8.** a deposit of $145.50

Find the absolute value.

9. $|-11|$ **10.** $|13|$ **11.** $-|3 \cdot 5|$ **12.** $|-2 + (-5)|$ **13.** $-|-10|$ **14.** $|2.1|$

Simplify.

15. $-3 + 5$ **16.** $8 - 10$ **17.** $(-\frac{1}{3})(3)$ **18.** $-55 \div 11$

19. $-2 + 7 + (-6)$ **20.** $-3 - (-11)$ **21.** $(-2)(-7)(-1)$ **22.** $\frac{-7}{-7}$

Simplify using mixed operations.

23. $7^2 - (-1)^2$ **24.** $-2 + 4 \cdot -12$ **25.** $9 - 6^2$ **26.** $(6 + (-2) - 3^2) \div -5$

Simplify by combining like terms.

27. $-7x + 9x$ **28.** $-3x - 5y + 2x + 10y$ **29.** $-4(5x - 11) - (6 + 2x)$

30. You drove 256 miles in 4 hours. What was your average speed?

Name _____   Date _____

Unit 2 Test   **Using Rules of Algebra**

Write each set of numbers in increasing order.

1. $-\frac{1}{3}$, 0, -4, 2, 5   **2.** 7, 2, -7, -2, $\frac{1}{2}$ **3.** $-3\frac{1}{2}$, 6, -12, 5, 11

Give the coordinate of each point graphed. Then give its opposite.

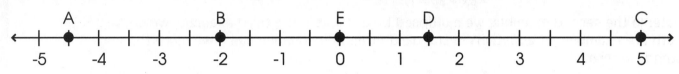

4. A   **5.** B   **6.** C   **7.** D   **8.** E

Write a situation to represent each number.

9. -8 _____

10. $305.25 _____

Compare. Use **<**, **>**, or **=** to make each statement true.

11. $|4.5|$ _____ $|-4.5|$ **12.** $|9|$ _____ $|13|$ **13.** $|-15|$ _____ $|-8|$

Evaluate when $x = -3$, $y = -1$, and $z = 4$.

14. $x + y$ **15.** $x + y + z$ **16.** $y + z$ **17.** $x - y$ **18.** $x - y - z$

Multiply or divide.

19. $\frac{-10}{5}$ **20.** $-21 \div 0$ **21.** $(-2)(-1)(6)$ **22.** $\frac{-6}{7} \div \frac{1}{7}$ **23.** $(\frac{1}{8})(-8)$

Simplify.

24. $-3 + 4 \cdot 3^2$ **25.** $-(4)^2 - (-1)^3$ **26.** $2((-5 + 7)^2 - 9) \div 2$

27. What is the difference between a rate and a ratio? Give an example of both.

Standard form of linear equations

A linear equation written in the form of $ax + By = C$, where a, B, and C are all real numbers, is the standard form of an equation of any line. Any equation can be transformed into this standard form simply by adding or subtracting like terms on both sides of the equation.

$7y + 2x = 10$ $\qquad$ $10 - 8y = 6x$ $\qquad$ $9 + 9x = 11y$

$2x + 7y = 10$ $\qquad$ $10 - 10 - 8y = 6x - 10$ $\qquad$ $9 - 9 + 9x = 11y - 9$

$\qquad\qquad\qquad$ $-8y - 6x = 6x - 6x - 10$ $\qquad$ $9x - 11y = 11y - 11y - 9$

$\qquad\qquad\qquad$ $(-1)(-6x - 8y) = (-1)(-10)$ $\qquad$ $9x - 11y = -9$

$\qquad\qquad\qquad$ $6x + 8y = 10$

Note: In the second example, we multiplied by a -1 and in the third example, we chose not to. Both are examples of equations in standard form. Any equation can have more than one standard form.

1. Write the standard form of the equation of a line.

Tell whether each equation below is written in standard form. Write **yes** or **no**.

2. $3x - y = 10$ $\qquad$ **3.** $-7x + 10y = -14$ $\qquad$ **4.** $y = 3x - 9$

5. $8x = y - 4$ $\qquad$ **6.** $-6x - 10y = 5$ $\qquad$ **7.** $12 = -2x + 4y$

Write each equation in standard form.

8. $-3y - 6x = 11$ $\qquad$ **9.** $2x - 4y - 14 = 0$

Add or Subtract like terms on both sides of the equation.

10. $7x = -3y + 5$ $\qquad$ **11.** $y = 3x + 8$

12. $-9 + 8x = -10y$ $\qquad$ **13.** $-7y - 10x + 11 = 0$

14. $7y + 2x = 12$ $\qquad$ **15.** $y = -x - 15$

Slope-intercept form of linear equations

Writing Linear Equations

Linear equations are equations of lines. A linear equation written in slope-intercept form is $y = mx + b$, where m is the slope of the line and b is the y-intercept. The y-intercept is the point at which the line crosses the y-axis.

$y = 3x + 2$	$y = -5x + 1$	$y = x - 7$	$y = -8x - 10$
$m = 3$, y-int. $= 2$	$m = -5$, y-int. $= 1$	$m = 1$, y-int. $= -7$	$m = -8$, y-int. $= -10$

Equations written in standard form can be put in slope-intercept form simply by adding or subtracting terms from either side of the equations.

$$3x + y = 12$$
$$3x - 3x + y = 12 - 3x$$
$$y = -3x + 12$$

$$-7x - y = 4$$
$$-7x + 7x - y = 4 + 7x$$
$$-y = 7x + 4$$
$$(-1)-y = (-1)(7x + 4)$$
$$y = -7x - 4$$

$$6x - 2y = 10$$
$$6x - 6x - 2y = 10 - 6x$$
$$\frac{-2y}{-2} = \frac{10}{-2} - \frac{6x}{-2}$$
$$y = -5 + 3x$$
$$y = 3x - 5$$

1. Write the slope-intercept form of the equation of a line.

State the slope and the y-intercept of each line.

2. $y = 2x + 5$

3. $y = x - 10$

4. $y = -x + 4$

5. $y = -3x + 7$

6. $y = -5x$

7. $y = 5$

Put each equation in slope-intercept form.

8. $3x + y = 10$

9. $7x - y = -12$

10. $-7x - y = -5$

11. $-3y = 12 + 3x$

12. $4y = 4x + 8$

13. $x + 2y = 16$

14. $-2x + 8y = -8$

15. $-12y = 24x + 12$

Point-slope form of linear equations

The point-slope form of an equation of a line is $y - y_1 = m(x - x_1)$, where (x_1, y_1) is a point on the line and m is the slope of the line. When using this form, be sure to see the difference between (x_1, y_1) and (x, y). The coordinates x_1 and y_1 represent a particular point on the line, and the coordinates x and y represent any other point on that same line.

$$y - 2 = -1(x - 3) \qquad y + 7 = 8(x - 5) \qquad y - 10 = -6(x + 2)$$

Any equation can be put in point-slope form given a point on the line and the slope of the line.

$(5, 3), m = 2$	$(8, -2), m = 6$	$(-7, 9), m = -10$
$y - 3 = 2(x - 5)$	$y - (-2) = 6(x - 8)$	$y - 9 = -10(x - (-7))$
	$y + 2 = 6(x - 8)$	$y - 9 = -10(x + 7)$

note: In example 2 and 3, the given point had negative numbers. Since the point-slope form has two minus signs, the $y - y_1$ in the second example turned to $y + y_1$ and the $x - x_1$ in the third example turned to $x + x_1$. Be sure to account for these signs whenever you have a point (x_1, y_1) that involves negative numbers.

1. Write the point-slope form of the equation of a line.

Write **yes** or **no** to state whether each line is in the point-slope form.

2. $x - 5 = -2(y + 7)$

3. $8 - x = 5(4 - y)$

4. $y + 7 = 8(x - 1)$

5. $y - 10 = 3(x - 2)$

6. $y - 12 = -7(x + 5)$

7. $6 - y = -12(2 + x)$

Write an equation of the line that passes through the point and has the given slope. Put each equation in point-slope form.

8. $(2, 3), m = 4$

9. $(-5, -4), m = -8$

10. $(-5, 7), m = -3$

11. $(2, 4), m = -1$

12. $(-1, 2), m = 1$

13. $(6, -8), m = 2$

14. $(1, -1), m = \frac{1}{2}$

15. $(-4, -1), m = -\frac{1}{2}$

Linear equations using slope-intercept form

Writing Linear Equations

Remember, the slope-intercept form of a linear equation is $y = mx + b$, where m is the slope and b is the y-intercept. To write an equation of a line in this form, you would need the slope and the y-intercept of the line.

$$m = 2, y\text{-int.} = 4 \qquad m = -4, y\text{-int.} = -9 \qquad m = -1, y\text{-int.} = 11$$
$$y = mx + b \qquad\qquad y = mx + b \qquad\qquad y = mx + b$$
$$y = 2x + 4 \qquad\qquad y = -4x - 9 \qquad\qquad y = -x + 11$$

Note: In the third example, the slope is -1. Only *-x is written*. If the slope was 1, only *x would be written*. The coefficient 1 is simply understood to be there and usually is not written.

State the slope and *y*-intercept of each line below.

1. $y = -2x + 5$

2. $y = -8x$

3. $2 + y = -x$

4. $-9 + y = x$

5. $y = 7$

6. $y = 2x - 7$

7. $-6 + y = 4x$

8. $y = -x$

Write an equation of the line given its slope and *y*-intercept.

9. $m - 1, y\text{-int.} - -1$

10. $m - 0, y\text{-int.} = 7$

11. $m = -2, y\text{-int.} = -5$

12. $m = -\frac{1}{4}, y\text{-int.} = -3$

13. $m = \frac{1}{2}, y\text{-int.} = -6$

14. $m = -1, y\text{-int.} = 8$

15. $m = 1, y\text{-int.} = 2$

16. $m = 4, y\text{-int.} = 0$

17. What is the name of the $y = mx + b$ form of an equation of a line?

18. Is 7 the *x*-intercept or *y*-intercept of the line $y = -4x + 7$?

Linear equations given the slope and a point

Remember the slope-intercept form of an equation is $y = mx + b$, where m is the slope and b is the y-intercept. This form can be helpful in finding the equation of a line given the slope and any point on the line. The point (x, y) is just substituted in for x and y in the equation. Also substituting the value of m in for the slope, you are left with b, which is the y-intercept. Once the slope and the y-intercept are found, the equation of the given line can be written.

point $(5, 4)$, $m = 2$

$y = mx + b$

$4 = 2(5) + b$

$4 = 10 + b$

$-6 = b$

point $(-2, 3)$, $m = 4$

$y = mx + b$

$3 = 4(-2) + b$

$3 = -8 + b$

$11 = b$

Solve each equation for b.

1. $-3 = \frac{1}{2}(-4) + b$

2. $4 = (-\frac{2}{3})(9) + b$

3. $-2 = (-\frac{3}{2})(-\frac{8}{3}) + b$

4. $-5 = 7(-2) + b$

5. $6 = (7)(-1) + b$

6. $7 = -9(-2) + b$

Given the point and slope of each line, find the y-intercept.

7. $(-4, 7)$, $m = 3$

8. $(0, 1)$, $m = 4$

9. $(-4, -2)$, $m = -1$

10. $(-3, -5)$, $m = -2$

11. $(4, 3)$, $m = -3$

12. $(3, 1)$, $m = -3$

State the equation of each line using its slope and y-intercept in problems 7–12. Write the equation in slope-intercept form.

13.

14.

15.

16.

17.

18.

Write the slope-intercept form of the equation of a line that passes through the point and has the given slope.

19. $m = \frac{2}{3}$, point $(3, 5)$

20. $m = -2$, point $(-2, 6)$

Linear equations given two points

To find any equation of a line, the slope of the line must be found. When just two points are given and the equation of the line that contains these points must be found, the first step to take is to find the slope of the line. The equation for the slope, m, of a line given two points is

$$m = \frac{\text{rise}}{\text{run}} = \frac{y_2 - y_1}{x_2 - x_1}, \text{ where } (x_1, y_1), \text{ and } (x_2, y_2) \text{ are the}$$

given points on the same line.

points (5, -7) and (7, 5)

$$m = \frac{\text{rise}}{\text{run}} = \frac{5 - (-7)}{7 - 5} = \frac{12}{2} = 6$$

$$m = 6$$

points (2, 0) and (-4, -3)

$$m = \frac{\text{rise}}{\text{run}} = \frac{-3 - 0}{-4 - 2} = \frac{-3}{-6} = \frac{1}{2}$$

$$m = \frac{1}{2}$$

Now that the slopes are found given the sets of points above, move ahead and find the equation of each line. Choose one point from each example and use the slope found in its example to find the y-intercept. Once the y-intercept is found, you have everything to write the equation of each line.

point (7, 5), $m = 6$
$$y = mx + b$$
$$5 = 6(7) + b$$
$$5 = 42 + b$$
$$-37 = b$$

point (2, 0), $m = \frac{1}{2}$
$$y = mx + b$$
$$0 = \frac{1}{2}(2) + b$$
$$0 = 1 + b$$
$$-1 = b$$

The equation of the line is $y = 6x - 37$.

The equation of the line is $y = \frac{1}{2}x - 1$.

Find the slope of each line given each set of points.

1. (-1, -1), (2, 8)

2. (3, 1), (-3, 5)

3. (6, -5), (1, 5)

4. (1, 2), (2, 4)

5. (7, 4), (-2, -5)

6. (1, 8), (8, 8)

Write the slope-intercept form of the equation of each line that passes through the given points above.

7.

8.

9.

10.

11.

12.

Write the slope-intercept form of the equation of the line that passes through each set of points.

13. (-3, -3), (-6, 0)

14. (1, 1), (-3, 1)

15. (-1, 4), (-3, 8)

Review of Unit 3

Topics covered:
Standard Form of Linear Equations	Linear Equations Using Slope-Intercept Form
Slope-Intercept Form of Linear Equations	Linear Equations Given the Slope and a Point
Point-Slope Form of Linear Equations	Linear Equations Given Two Points

1. Write the standard form of a linear equation.

2. Write the slope-intercept form of a linear equation.

3. Write the point-slope form of a linear equation.

4. Explain what is needed to write an equation in slope-intercept form.

5. Explain how to write an equation in slope-intercept form given the slope and a point.

6. Explain how to write an equation in slope-intercept form given two points.

Find the slope of each line that contains each set of points. Then write an equation in point-slope form using one of the points and the slope.

7. $(4, -7), (6, 9)$ 8. $(-2, -1), (-3, -5)$ 9. $(3, 2), (7, 6)$

Write an equation of the line in slope-intercept form given the slope and a point on the line. State the y-intercept of each line.

10. $(3, -6), m = -8$ 11. $(-4, -3), m = -1$ 12. $(-5, 2), m = 7$

Write an equation of the line in slope-intercept form given two points on the line. State the slope and y-intercept.

13. $(-2, 1), (7, 10)$ 14. $(4, -2), (6, -6)$ 15. $(0, 4), (-2, -10)$

Unit 3 Test   **Writing Linear Equations**

State the form of each equation of a line: **standard**, **slope-intercept**, or **point-slope** form.

1. $3x - 5y = 10$

2. $y = -7x + 4$

3. $(y - 5) = 4(x - 6)$

4. What two things are needed to be able to write an equation in slope-intercept form?

5. What is needed to be able to find the slope of a line? Explain how to find the slope of a line once you have what you need.

Name the slope and *y*-intercept in each equation of a line.

6. $2x - y = 5$

7. $y = -3x - 2$

8. $5x + y - 12 = 0$

Write an equation of a line in slope-intercept form that passes through the given point and has the given slope. State each *y*-intercept.

9. $(7, -9)$, $m = -4$

10. $(5, -6)$, $m = 4$

11. $(2, -1)$, $m = -2$

12. $(-3, -2)$, $m = -2$

13. $(-1, 8)$, $m = -3$

14. $(-6, -2)$, $m = 5$

Write an equation of a line in point-slope form given two points on the line. State the slope and *y*-intercept of each line.

15. $(12, -10)$, $(8, -2)$

16. $(5, -7)$, $(-6, 4)$

17. $(-3, -2)$, $(-1, 2)$

Solving equations by adding or subtracting

Solving Linear Equations

When solving equations for a particular variable, use the addition or the subtraction property of equality. The addition property means that adding the same number to both sides of an equation will produce an equivalent equation.

$x - 3 = 5$ Solve for x by adding 3 to both sides of the equation.

$x - 3 + 3 = 5 + 3$

$x = 8$ When 3 is added to both sides, -3 and 3 gives a result of 0, leaving x by itself. Therefore, $x = 8$ is the answer.

The subtraction property means that subtracting the same number from both sides of an equation will produce an equivalent equation.

$x + 3 = 5$ Solve for x by subtracting 3 from both sides of the equation.

$x + 3 - 3 = 5 - 3$

$x = 2$ When 3 is subtracted from both sides, 3 – 3 gives a result of 0, leaving x by itself. Therefore, $x = 2$ is the answer.

Answers can be checked by substituting the value of x back into the equation. This is to make sure the value of x makes a true sentence when substituted into the original equation.

$x - 3 = 5, x = 8$ $x + 3 = 5, x = 2$

$8 - 3 = 5$ $2 + 3 = 5$

$5 = 5$ (makes a true statement) $5 = 5$ (makes a true statement)

Solve each equation for x. Check your answers.

1. $x - 10 = 23$ **2.** $6 + x = -11$ **3.** $-13 = -6 + x$

4. $7 = 14 + x$ **5.** $8 = x + 9$ **6.** $x - 5 = -5$

7. $x + 3 = 12$ **8.** $7 + x = 7$ **9.** $7 + x = -7$

10. $-2 = x - 5$ **11.** $x + 4 = -15$ **12.** $9 = x + 12$

Translate each problem into an equation. Solve each equation.

13. Ten more than a number is 38. Find the number.

14. The price of a coat decreased by $40 has the discount price of $90. Find the original cost.

Solving equations by multiplying or dividing   **Solving Linear Equations**

When solving equations for a particular variable, use the multiplication or division property of equality. The multiplication property means that multiplying the same nonzero number by both sides of the equation will produce an equivalent equation.

$\frac{x}{7} = 3$ Multiply both sides of the equation by 7 to get x by itself.

$(7)(\frac{x}{7}) = (7)(3)$ Check $\frac{21}{7} = 3$

$x = 21$ $3 = 3$ true statement

Thus, the solution is 21.

The division property means that dividing both sides of the equation by the same nonzero number will produce an equivalent equation.

$-5x = 20$ Divide both sides of the equation by -5 to get x by itself.

$\frac{-5x}{-5} = \frac{20}{-5}$ Check $-5(-4) = 20$

$x = -4$ $20 = 20$ true statement

Thus, the solution is -4.

Solve each equation for x. Check your answers.

1. $5x = 35$ **2.** $18 = -3x$ **3.** $-7x = 49$

4. $-\frac{1}{3}x = 6$ **5.** $-5x = -20$ **6.** $-\frac{5}{8}x = 10$

7. $\frac{1}{4}x = 2$ **8.** $\frac{2}{3}x = 8$ **9.** $4 = -\frac{x}{5}$

10. $-4x = 48$ **11.** $\frac{x}{3} = -5$ **12.** $-6x = 24$

Translate each problem into an equation. Solve each equation.

13. Joe worked 21 hours on his class project. He worked 3 times as long as Mary did. How long did Mary work on her project?

14. Eight times a number is -96. Find the number.

15. John spent $\frac{2}{3}$ of his savings on a new radio. The radio cost $80. How much was John's savings before he bought the radio?

Name _____   Date _____

Solving equations using multiple steps

Solving Linear Equations

When solving equations for a particular variable, sometimes you need to use more than one of the properties of equality.

$3x - 2 = 7$

$3x - 2 + 2 = 7 + 2$ Add 2 to both sides of the equation.

$\frac{3x}{3} = \frac{9}{3}$ Now, divide both sides of the equation by 3.

$x = 3$ Check $3(3) - 2 = 7$
$9 - 2 = 7$
$7 = 7$ true statement

Thus, the solution is 3.

Here are some steps to follow when solving multi-step equations.

1. Simplify both sides of the equation (if needed).
2. Use the addition or subtraction property of equality to isolate terms containing the variable.
3. Use the multiplication or the division property of equality to further isolate the variable.
4. Check the solution.

Solve each equation for x. Check your answers.

1. $6x - 3 = 21$

2. $6 + \frac{x}{4} = -1$

3. $18 - 3x = -12$

4. $7 + 2x = -13$

5. $-4 = 7x + 8 - 8x$

6. $13 = 9 - \frac{x}{5}$

7. $-7 - x = -5$

8. $5x + 9 - 4x = 12$

9. $-8x - 13 = 19$

10. $-3 = -5 - 2x$

11. $\frac{1}{3}x + 9 = 15$

12. $-7 = 3x - 15 - 7x$

Translate each problem into an equation. Solve each equation.

13. Thirty-two is 7 less than 3 times a number. Find the number.

14. Negative twenty-five is 4 times a number increased by 7. Find the number.

15. Twelve pounds less than twice Jane's weight is 270 pounds. What is Jane's weight?

Solving equations with variables on both sides

Solving Linear Equations

Often, equations with a variable on both sides of the equation need to be solved. This requires one additional step of getting the variable on one side only.

$4x - 1 = 2x + 7$

$4x - 2x - 1 = 2x - 2x + 7$ Get the variable on one side of the equation.

$2x - 1 = 7$ Now, solve for x using the properties of equality.

$2x - 1 + 1 = 7 + 1$

$\frac{2x}{2} = \frac{8}{2}$ Check $4(4) - 1 = 2(4) + 7$

$x = 4$ $16 - 1 = 8 + 7$

$15 = 15$ true statement

Thus, the solution is 4.

note: Combine the variables on the side of the equation with the greater variable coefficient, in order to avoid solving an equation with a variable which has a negative coefficient.

Solve each equation for x. Check your answers.

1. $9x - 12 = 3x$

2. $8x - 12 = 15x - 4x$

3. $11 + 6x = 2x - 13$

4. $-5x = 9 - 2x$

5. $-8x - 10 = 4x + 14$

6. $10x - 5 = 21 - 3x$

7. $-12x = 14 - 5x$

8. $19 - 3x = 21 + x$

9. $4x + 12 = -3x - 6 + 4x$

Translate each problem into an equation. Solve each equation.

10. Twice Beth's daily pay is the same as her daily pay increased by $45. Find Beth's daily pay.

11. A number decreased by 12 is the same as 3 times the number. Find the number.

12. The temperature, increased by 65°, is the same as 5 times the temperature decreased by 15°. Find the temperature.

Solving equations with parentheses

Equations often contain parentheses. When asked to solve equations such as these, first use the distributive property and then combine like terms, solving the rest of the equation using the properties of equality.

$6x - 4(2 - 3x) = 28$ Use the distributive property to begin simplifying.

$6x - 8 + 12x = 28$ Combine like terms.

$18x - 8 = 28$ Solve equation for x.

$18x - 8 + 8 = 28 + 8$

$\dfrac{18x}{18} = \dfrac{36}{18}$ Check $6(2) - 4[2 - 3(2)] = 28$

$x = 2$ $12 - 4(2 - 6) = 28$

Thus, the solution is 2. $12 + 16 = 28$

$28 = 28$ true statement

Use the distributive property to remove the parentheses.

1. $3(5x - 10)$

2. $(6x + 5)(-2)$

3. $-4(x - 6) = 2(7 - 7x)$

4. $-5(2 - 5x)$

5. $(-12 - 7x)(4)$

6. $8(-9x + 4) = -3(6x + 9)$

Solve each equation for x. Check your answers.

7. $3(x + 7) = 30$

8. $2(x + 3) = 12 - x$

9. $-(x + 7) -5 = 4(x + 3) - 6x$

10. $-5(x + 4) = 20$

11. $5(5 - x) = 4(x - 5)$

12. $5(x - 1) = 2x + 4(x - 1)$

Translate each problem into an equation. Solve each equation.

13. Four times the sum of a number and 7 is 44 less than the number. Find the number.

14. Sixteen more than a number is the same as 8 times the sum of the number and 9.

Name _____   Date _____

Problem solving with formulas

When problem solving in algebra, it is a good idea to have a general problem-solving plan. This can help lay the groundwork for finding the solution to any given word problem.

Joan is going to take a bike trip. She plans to ride 9 miles in 45 minutes. At what rate (mi/h) must she travel?

Plan: Use the formula $d = rt$, where d is the distance, r is the rate, and t is the time. First, change 45 minutes to terms of hours which is $\frac{45}{60} = \frac{3}{4}$. So, the time is equal to $\frac{3}{4}$ of an hour. Now, solve using the formula $d = rt$.

$$d = rt$$
$$9\left(\frac{4}{3}\right) = r\left(\frac{3}{4}\right)\left(\frac{4}{3}\right)$$
$$\frac{36}{3} = r$$
$$r = 12 \text{ miles per hour}$$

Thus, 12 mi/h is the rate at which Joan must travel to ride 9 miles in 45 minutes.

1. Use the formula $d = rt$ to find the average speed of driving 330 miles in $5\frac{1}{2}$ hours.

A school drama club is putting on a play. Its expenses will be $300. Use the formula $p = nt - e$, (p is profit, n is number of tickets, t is price per ticket, e is expenses) to answer questions 2–5.

2. How many tickets must be sold at $3 each to make $1,500 profit?

3. If the drama club expects to sell approximately 600 tickets, what should it charge for each ticket to make $1,800 profit?

4. If the drama club sells 500 tickets at $2.50 each, what will be its profit?

5. If the drama club expects to sell only 450 tickets at $2.50 each, by how much would it have to lower expenses to make $1,000 profit?

Review of Unit 4

Topics covered:

Solving Equations by Adding or Subtracting	Solving Equations with Variables on Both Sides
Solving Equations by Multiplying or Dividing	Solving Equations with Parentheses
Solving Equations Using Multiple Steps	Problem Solving with Formulas

Solve each equation for x.

1. $x + 5 = 10$

2. $14 + 3x = x - 16$

3. $12 + x = 15 + 4x$

4. $-x - 3 + 2x = 10$

5. $12x + 2 - 3x = 10 - (x - 2)$

6. $3(x + 4) - 6x = 2(4 - 2x)$

7. $(-6x - 2)4 = -22x$

8. $7x + 12 = -10x - 22$

Translate each problem into an equation. Solve each equation.

9. If Steve's age is decreased by 12 years, and that difference is multiplied by 3, the result is 24 years. Find Steve's age.

10. Ten more than 6 times Harold's age is the same as 4 times his age increased by 40. Find Harold's age.

11. Using $d = rt$, find d for $r = 65$ mi/h and $t = 9$ hours.

12. Using $p = nt - e$, find the number of tickets (n) sold if the profit (p) is $1,350, the price of a ticket (t) is $8, and the expenses ($e$) is $250.

Unit 4 Test

Solve each equation for x. Check each solution.

1. $x - 15 = 12$

2. $x - 4 = -6x + 5 + 5x - 1$

3. $-11 = -4 + x$

4. $2(x - 2) = -5(3 - x) - 1$

5. $-\frac{1}{3}x - 5 = 6$

6. $-3x - 10 = 5x + 6$

7. $-3x + 7 - 2x = 4x - 2$

8. $\frac{2}{3}x = -10$

Translate each problem into an equation. Solve each equation.

9. Five less than twice the temperature is 21°F. Find the temperature.

10. Three times Jan's salary is the same as her salary increased by $110.

11. If 4 times a number is decreased by 9 and then increased by 12, the result is 5 less than 2 times the number. Find the number.

12. Using $d = rt$, find r if $d = 350$ miles and $t = 5$ hours.

13. Using $p = nt - e$, find the number of tickets sold (n) if the profit (p) is $350, the price of a ticket (t) is $3, and the expenses ($e$) is $250.

Graphing one-variable equations

Graphing Linear Equations

One-variable equations graph into straight lines. In a coordinate plane, the following is true:

1. The graph of $x = a$ is a vertical line, where a is the first coordinate of the point at which the line crosses the x-axis.

2. The graph of $y = b$ is a horizontal line, where b is the second coordinate of the point at which the line crosses the y-axis.

The graph of $x = 2$ crosses the x-axis at the point $(2, 0)$.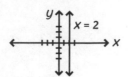

The graph of $y = 5$ crosses the y-axis at the point $(0, 5)$.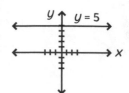

note: The graph of a vertical line will have all the same x-coordinates and the y-coordinates will vary. The graph of a horizontal line will have x-coordinates that vary and all of the same y-coordinates.

Match each equation with its graph.

1. $x = -2$ **2.** $y = -2$ **3.** $x = 1$ **4.** $y = 1$

A. 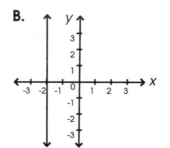   **B.** 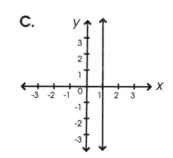   **C.**   **D.**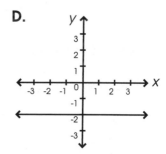

Sketch each line on a coordinate plane. State the point at which both lines intersect.

5. $x = 7, y = -2$ **6.** $x = -5, y = 3$ **7.** $x = 1, y = -1$ **8.** $x = -5, y = -3$

Tell whether the point lies on the line. Write **yes** or **no**.

9. $(-7, 4), x = 4$ **10.** $(5, -2), y = -2$ **11.** $(9, -6), x = 9$ **12.** $(6, 5), y = 6$

Write an equation for each graph. Sketch the graph.

13. a line whose x-coordinate of each point is -1

14. a line whose y-coordinate of each point is 4

Graphing two-variable equations

The graph of a linear equation with two variables, $ax + By = C$, is a straight line. The graph of an equation is the collection of all points (x, y) that are solutions of the equation. Two or more points are needed to graph a line. To construct a graph of a line, start by using a table of values. Follow these steps.

1. Choose several x-values.
2. Substitute these x-values into the equation.
3. Find the corresponding y-value.
4. Graph each point.
5. Connect the points to show the graph of the line containing all of these points.

Sketch the graph of $2x + y = 7$.

First, solve for y. $y = -2x + 7$.

Choose several values for x and solve for y to find some solutions of this equation.

When $x = 2$, $y = 3$. So $(2, 3)$ is a solution.
When $x = 3$, $y = 1$. So $(3, 1)$ is a solution.
When $x = 0$, $y = 7$. So $(0, 7)$ is a solution.

Now, graph the line $2x + y = 7$ using these three points that lie on the line.

Tell whether each point is a solution to the equation. Write **yes** or **no**.

1. $2x - 4y = 7$; $(6, 1)$

2. $-x + y = -6$; $(-5, -11)$

3. $-3x + 5y = -12$; $(-1, -3)$

4. $8y - 3x = 5$; $(6, 3)$

Solve for y in each equation. Give three solutions to each equation.

5. $x - y = -5$

6. $-2x + y = 7$

7. $3x - 4y = 12$

8. $-5x + 3y = -15$

Sketch the graph of each equation by finding three solutions to each equation.

9. $4x + 3y = -24$

10. $y = -3x + 1$

11. $y = 2x - 5$

12. $-2x - 3y = 6$

Graphing using intercepts

Using the standard form of a linear equation, $ax + By = C$,

1. The x-intercept of a line is the x-value when $y = 0$. To find the x-intercept, let $y = 0$ and solve $ax = C$ for x.
2. The y-intercept of a line is the y-value when $x = 0$. To find the y-intercept, let $x = 0$ and solve $By = C$ for y.

The intercepts of a line provide a quick and easy way to graph any line.

Graph $3x + 4y = 12$ using the intercepts.

Let $y = 0$. The x-intercept is 4. It can be found at the point (4, 0).
Let $x = 0$. The y-intercept is 3. It can be found at the point (0, 3).

Plotting these two points on the graph and drawing a line through them gives the graph of the line $3x + 4y = 12$.

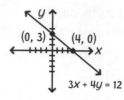

Use each graph below to find the x-intercept and the y-intercept of the line.

1.
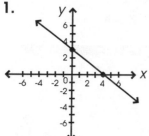

x-int. = _____

y-int. = _____

2.
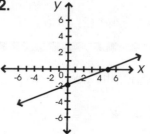

x-int. = _____

y-int. = _____

3.
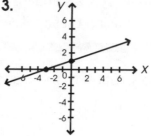

x-int. = _____

y-int. = _____

4.
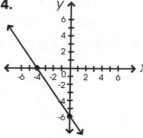

x-int. = _____

y-int. = _____

Sketch each line with the given intercepts.

5. x-intercept = 5
y-intercept = -2

6. x-intercept = -1
y-intercept = 3

7. x-intercept = -4
y-intercept = -3

8. x-intercept = 2
y-intercept = 4

Find the x-intercept and y-intercept of each line. Sketch the graph.

9. $x + 2y = 6$

10. $-3x - 4y = 12$

11. $-9x + 4y = -36$

12. $5x - 3y = -15$

Slope of a line

The slope of a line is the number of units a line rises or falls for each unit of horizontal change from left to right on its graph. The slope of a line is represented by the letter m and can be found given two points (x_1, y_1) and (x_2, y_2) on the line using the following formula.

$$m = \frac{rise}{run} = \frac{y_2 - y_1}{x_2 - x_1}$$

If the slope is greater than 0 (which is positive), then the line rises from left to right.
If the slope is less than 0 (which is negative), then the line falls from left to right.
If the slope is equal to 0, then the line is horizontal.
If the slope is undefined, then the line is vertical.

Find the slope of the line passing through the points (-5, 6) and (-3, 10).

$$m = \frac{rise}{run} = \frac{y_2 - y_1}{x_2 - x_1} = \frac{10 - 6}{-3 - (-5)} = \frac{4}{-3 + 5} = \frac{4}{2} = \frac{2}{1} = 2$$

Thus, since the slope is a positive 2, then we know the line rises from left to right.

Determine whether the line **rises from left to right, falls from left to right,** is **vertical**, or is **horizontal,** given the following slopes.

1. $m = 2$

2. $m = -5$

3. $m = 6$

4. $m =$ undefined

5. $m = 0$

6. $m = -7$

Find the slope of the line that passes through each set of points.

7. (5, 4), (6, 9)

8. (-3, 4), (-1, 2)

9. (-6, -3), (-2, 9)

10. (-2, -1), (0, 3)

11. (6, -5), (3, 10)

12. (7, 8), (1, -16)

Sketch the line by plotting the points. Find the slope of the line passing through the points.

13. (0, 0), (2, 4)

14. (-1, -2), (-3, 6)

15. (4, -5), (5, -10)

16. (-2, 0), (-5, 6)

Graphing using slope-intercept form

To graph a line using its slope and y-intercept, the first thing to do is put the equation in its slope-intercept form, $y = mx + b$. Then m is the slope of the line and b is the y-intercept. Here are the steps to graph a line using its slope and y-intercept.

1. Put the line equation in slope-intercept form.
2. Find the slope and y-intercept.
3. Graph the y-intercept.
4. Graph the slope. Start at the y-intercept point, move up or down, then right or left (rise over the run).

Graph the line $5x + y = 7$.

Put the line in slope-intercept form. $y = -5x + 7$

Find the slope and y-intercept. $m = -5$, y-intercept = 7

Now, graph $(0, 7)$. Move from this point down 5 places and then to the right 1, since the slope is $-\frac{5}{1}$. The graph answer point is $(1, 2)$. Thus, you have the graph of the line $5x + y = 7$.

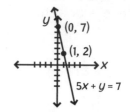

Solve each equation for y.

1. $7x - 4y = 0$

2. $y + 18 = 0$

3. $3x - 2y = -12$

4. $-8x + y = 4$

5. $-4x - 5y = 40$

6. $7x + 2y = -10$

Find the slope and y-intercept of each line.

7. $y = -3x + 5$

8. $y = 7x + 11$

9. $2y - x = 3x - 4$

10. $y = -2 + 4x$

11. $x + y = 2x - 5$

12. $x - y = -9$

Sketch the two lines on the same coordinate plane. State the slope, x-intercept, and y-intercept of each line.

13. $y = -2x + 4$, $y = -2x - 3$

14. $y = x + 1$, $y = -x + 1$

15. $y = 3x + 3$, $y = -3x - 3$

16. $y = 5x$, $y = -5x$

Name _____   Date _____

Review of Unit 5

Topics covered:
  Graphing One-Variable Equations   Slope of a Line
  Graphing Two-Variable Equations   Graphing Using Slope-Intercept Form
  Graphing Using Intercepts

Sketch both lines on the same coordinate plane. State the point at which the two lines intersect.

1. $x = 5$, $y = -2$ **2.** $x = -2$, $y = 1$ **3.** $x = 3$, $y = 4$ **4.** $x = -4$, $y = -1$

Determine whether the point lies on the line. State **yes** or **no**.

5. $(-7, 2)$, $y = -7$ **6.** $(-4, -1)$, $x = -4$ **7.** $(3, -3)$, $x = -3$

Find three solutions to each equation. Sketch its graph.

8. $y = 4x - 5$ **9.** $x + y = -3$ **10.** $2x - y = 7$ **11.** $4x - 8y = -24$

Find the slope of the line passing through each set of points. Tell whether the line **rises from right to left, falls from right to left**, is **vertical**, or is **horizontal**.

12. $(7, 5)$, $(5, 7)$ **13.** $(-1, -3)$, $(-4, 9)$ **14.** $(5, -6)$, $(2, -9)$

Solve for y in each equation. State the slope and y-intercept. Sketch the graph.

15. $3x - y = -4$ **16.** $-2x + 2y = -6$ **17.** $-4x - 5y = 20$

Find the x-intercept and y-intercept of each line.

18. $x - y = -5$ **19.** $-3x + 7y = -21$ **20.** $5x - 8y = 40$ **21.** $-x - 3y = 15$

Graph each line. State the method you used and explain why.

22. $y = -5x - 2$ **23.** $3x - 5y = 15$ **24.** $6x - y = 7$

Unit 5 Test Graphing Linear Equations

1. Sketch the graphs of $x = -2$ and $y = 5$. Then state the point at which these two lines intersect.

2. Solve $3x + 4y = -24$ for y. Give three solutions to this equation and use these points to sketch its graph.

3. Write an equation of a line whose x-coordinates are all 7. Give three points on this line.

4. Is $(4, -2)$ on the graph of $-3x - y = 10$? Explain why or why not.

Find the x-intercept and y-intercept in each equation. Sketch the line.

5. $y = -6x - 3$

6. $5x - 2y = -10$

7. $2x - y = -8$

Sketch each line which passes through the two points given. State the slope of the line and whether the line **rises from right to left**, **falls from right to left**, is **vertical**, or is **horizontal**.

8. $(-2, 4), (2, 4)$

9. $(-6, -3), (-3, 9)$

10. $(7, -9), (7, 12)$

Rewrite each equation in slope-intercept form. State the slope and y-intercept of each line. Sketch the graph.

11. $-7x + y = -1$

12. $2x - 2y = 4x - 10$

13. $4(2x + y) = 16$

Graph the following equations. State the method you chose to use and explain why.

14. $7x - 8y = -56$

15. $y = 2x - 6$

16. $-x - 7y = 14$

Translating English to algebra

It is important in algebra to be able to translate from a simple English sentence to a mathematical expression. In order to do this, follow three simple steps.

1. Identify the numbers that are unknowns.
2. Decide which of these numbers is going to be represented with a variable.
3. Determine how to represent the other numbers in terms of this variable.

Terry's age is 5 years less than twice Joe's age. Represent Terry and Joe's age in terms of x.

1. The two unknowns are Terry's age and Joe's age.
2. Joe's age is the basis of comparison because Terry's age is five years less than twice Joe's.
3. If Joe's age = x (basis of comparison), then Terry's age = $2x - 5$ (five years less than twice Joe's age).

Represent one of the unknowns below with a variable. Then represent the other unknown in terms of that variable.

1. Mary has won 4 more matches playing tennis than Sherri.

2. Joey has 3 less than 7 times as many stickers as John has.

3. The length of one board is 2 feet greater than twice the length of a second board.

4. This year's price of a football ticket has increased by one-third the price of a ticket last year.

5. Kent raised $75 less than 4 times what Sarah raised.

Danny has a box of pens consisting of the colors blue, black, and red. He has 8 less blue pens than black ones. He has the same number of black and red pens.

6. What color pens does Danny have the least of?

7. Let n = the number of black pens Danny has. Represent the number of blue pens in terms of n.

8. Represent the number of red pens in terms of n.

Name _____ Date _____

Problem solving with two or more numbers

When problem solving in algebra, it is important to follow five simple steps.

1. Identify the numbers that are unknowns.
2. Determine what is given in the problem.
3. Decide which of these given numbers in the problem can be represented by a variable and represent each of the other numbers in terms of this variable.
4. Write the actual equation.
5. Solve the equation for the unknowns.

A 36-inch ribbon used to tie a package is cut into two pieces. The first piece is 4 less than 3 times the second piece. Find the length of each piece of ribbon.

Let ℓ = the length of the second piece, then $3\ell - 4$ = the length of the first piece.

$$\ell + (3\ell - 4) = 36$$
$$4\ell - 4 = 36$$
$$4\ell = 40$$

$\ell = 10$ inches (length of second piece) $3(10) - 4 = 26$ inches (length of first piece)

Solve for the unknowns in each equation.

1. Steve's mom's age is 7 years less than 3 times Steve's age. The sum of their ages is 65 years. Find their ages.

2. Brianne's golf score is 8 more than Tim's score. The sum of their score is 96. Find each score.

3. The larger of two numbers is 8 times the smaller. The difference between them is 42. Find the numbers.

4. Shelley worked 12 more hours than Julie. They worked a total of 72 hours. How long did each girl work?

5. Eighty people are separated into 2 groups. The first group is 8 less than 3 times as large as the second. Find the number of people in each group.

6. Jake has 20 less than 3 times the amount of baseball cards Kevin has. Together they have 1,240 cards. How many baseball cards does each boy have?

Problem solving with perimeter

Applying Linear Equations

The perimeter of any figure is the sum of the lengths of its sides. Using this definition and what is known about problem solving in algebra, solve this problem.

A rectangle with a perimeter of 42 inches has a width of 3 less than twice its length. Find the length and width.

Let x = the length, then $2x - 3$ = the width.

Perimeter of a rectangle = $2\ell + 2w$

Substitute the givens into this equation and solve.

$42 = 2(x) + 2(2x - 3)$

$42 = 2x + 4x - 6$

$48 = 6x$

8 in. = x (the length) $2x - 3 = 2(8) - 3 = 13$ in. (the width)

Solve each problem.

1. A rectangle has a length of $4x$ and a width of $4x - 2$. Its perimeter is 12 inches. Find the length and width.

2. An equilateral triangle has a side of length $2x - 3$. Its perimeter is 33 inches. Find the length of each side.

3. A square has a side of length $2x$. Its perimeter is 56 inches. Find the length of each side.

4. The length of a rectangle is 4 times the width. The perimeter is 50 cm. Find the length and width.

5. The perimeter of a triangle is 25 inches. The first side is 6 inches longer than the second side. The third side is 5 inches shorter than twice the second side. Find the length of each side.

6. The length of each leg of an isosceles triangle is 8 cm less than 3 times the base. The perimeter is 33 cm. Find the length of each side.

7. An equilateral triangle has a side of length $2x - 3$. Its perimeter is 51 inches. Find the length of each side.

Solving equations with fractions

When solving equations with fractions, it is important to remember how to find the least common multiple and the least common denominator. The least common multiple of a group of fractions is the least number divisible by each of the fractions in the group. A least common multiple (LCM) can also be referred to as the least common denominator (LCD)—they are the same number.

Solve $\frac{2}{3}x - \frac{1}{4} = \frac{1}{2}$ The LCM, or LCD, is 12.

$12(\frac{2}{3}x - \frac{1}{4}) = \frac{1}{2}(12)$ Multiply both sides by 12.

$8x - 3 = 6$ Now, solve for x.

$8x = 9$

$x = \frac{9}{8}$ Check $\frac{2}{3}(\frac{9}{8}) - \frac{1}{4} = \frac{1}{2}$

Thus, the solution is $\frac{9}{8}$. $\frac{18}{24} - \frac{1}{4} = \frac{1}{2}$

$\frac{3}{4} - \frac{1}{4} = \frac{2}{4} = \frac{1}{2}$ true statement

Find the least common denominator of each group of fractions.

1. $\frac{1}{2}, \frac{1}{6}, \frac{5}{7}$

2. $\frac{2}{3}, \frac{3}{4}, \frac{1}{8}$

3. $\frac{5}{6}, \frac{3}{5}, \frac{2}{9}, \frac{1}{3}$

4. $\frac{3}{10}, \frac{2}{5}, \frac{1}{6}, \frac{2}{3}$

Solve each equation.

5. $\frac{1}{3}x - 2 = \frac{3}{4}$

6. $\frac{1}{2}x - 5 = \frac{1}{3}x + 8$

7. $\frac{3}{2}x + \frac{4}{3} = 9$

8. $\frac{3}{2}x - 6 = \frac{3}{5}x + 4$

9. $\frac{1}{4} - \frac{1}{6}x = \frac{3}{8}$

10. $\frac{1}{4}x - 1 = \frac{3}{5}x + 4$

Solve each problem.

11. Eight years more than $\frac{1}{2}$ of Johnny's age is 24 years. Find Johnny's age.

12. Five less than $\frac{3}{4}$ of a number equals twice the number. Find the number.

Solve each equation.

13. $\frac{3x+5}{12} - \frac{3}{4} = \frac{-2x-1}{3}$

14. $\frac{4x}{5} + \frac{3x-2}{10} = \frac{x+6}{4}$

Solving equations with decimals

The easiest way to solve equations that involve decimals is to multiply by powers of 10.

Solve $0.2x + 0.004 = 0.12$.

First, count the number of digits to the right of each decimal point.

0.2 has 1; 0.004 has 3; 0.12 has 2. The greatest number of digits to the right of any of these decimal points is 3; therefore, multiply both sides of the equation by 1,000 (or 10^3) and then solve for x.

$1,000(0.2x + 0.004) = 1,000(0.12)$ Check $0.2(0.58) + 0.004 = 0.12$

$200x + 4 = 120$ $0.116 + 0.004 = 0.12$

$200x = 116$ $0.12 = 0.12$ true statement

$x = 0.58$

Thus, the solution is 0.58.

State the power of 10 you would need to multiply by to eliminate each set of decimals. Round to the nearest hundredth when necessary.

1. 0.12, 0.4, 0.45

2. 0.34, 0.415, 0.002

3. 0.1156, 0.004, 0.012

Solve each equation.

4. $0.03x = 0.009$

5. $8.8 - 2.5x = 3.3$

6. $2.4x = 9.6$

7. $0.06 - 0.3x - 1.8$

8. $0.05x = 8.95$

9. $2.145 + 0.02x = 3.1005$

Solve each problem.

10. A number decreased by 0.08 of a number is 1.38. Find the number.

11. A number increased by 0.35 times the number is 0.675. Find the number.

Solving percent problems

Percent is used in many different situations in algebra. Percent is written %, meaning per hundred, or hundredths. A percent can be written three different ways.

$45\% = \frac{45}{100} = 0.45$ Each of these numbers represents a percent.

Three basic problems are used with percent.

1. What number is 35% of 50? $n = 0.35(50)$ Remember *of* means multiply.
                                       $n = 17.5$

2. 12 is 25% of what number? $12 = 0.25n$ Divide both sides by 0.25.
                                      $n = 48$

3. 15 is what percent of 60? $15 = p(60)$ Divide both sides by 60.
                                      $p = 0.25$
                                      $p = 25\%$

Percent can also apply to a word problem.

Find the percent of increase if Tom's salary was raised from $125 to $175.
percent of increase = amount of increase/original amount = $50/$125 = 0.4
Percent of increase of Tom's salary was 40%.

note: This type of problem can also be applied to percent of decrease. The formula would be percent of decrease = amount of decrease/original amount.

Write each percent in decimal form and in fraction form.

1. 47%   **2.** 15.5%   **3.** 33%   **4.** $8\frac{1}{2}\%$ **5.** 0.5%   **6.** $12\frac{3}{4}\%$

Write each fraction or decimal as a percent.

7. 0.35   **8.** $\frac{1}{2}$ **9.** 0.015   **10.** $\frac{3}{5}$ **11.** 1.5   **12.** $\frac{3}{8}$

Solve each problem.

13. What number is 20% of 80?   **14.** 25 is what percent of 200?

15. 18 is what percent of 90?   **16.** 60 is 37.5% of what number?

17. 45 is 40% of what number?   **18.** What number is $4\frac{1}{2}\%$ of 180?

19. A price increased from $12 to $15. Find the percent of increase.

20. A price is lowered from $25 to $15. Find the percent of decrease.

Problem solving using percents

Applying Linear Equations

Percent is used in problem solving in algebra in many different situations. Percent is related to sales tax, profit and cost, salary and commission, and the discount of an item. For example, the sale price of an item, which is the difference between the original price and the amount of discount, can be written as:

original price – amount of discount = sale price.

A jacket is on sale for 33% off. The sale price is $55. Find the original price of the jacket and the amount of discount.

Let p = original price, then the amount of discount will be $0.33p$.

Using the formula original price – amount of discount = sale price, solve.

$100(p - 0.33p) = (55)100$ Multiply both sides by 100 to get rid of the decimal.

$100p - 33p = 5500$

$67p = 5500$

$p = \$82.09$ (original price) Amount of discount = $0.33(82.09) = \$27.09$

Thus, the original price is $82.09, and the amount of discount is $27.09.

Solve each problem.

1. A couch is on sale for $750. The discount rate is 25%. Find the original price and the amount of discount.

2. Alisha bought a shirt with a marked price of $25.99. If the sales tax was 7%, what was the total price Alisha paid for the shirt?

3. George earned $450 last week, plus a 4% commission on his total sales. If his total earnings were $700, what were his sales?

4. The selling price of a car is $15,000. A 20% profit is included in this cost. Find the cost of the car.

5. Mark is paid 12% commission on all his sales, plus $4 an hour for a 40-hour week. If he earned $760, what were his total sales?

6. A TV's selling price is $550. Find the store's cost if the profit is 25% of the cost.

Name _____   Date _____

Review of Unit 6   **Applying Linear Equations**

Topics covered:
Translating English to Algebra   Solving Equations with Decimals
Problem Solving with Two or More Numbers   Solving Percent Problems
Problem Solving with Perimeter   Problem Solving Using Percents
Solving Equations with Fractions

Write an equation for each problem. Solve.

1. A number decreased by 54 is 6 less than 5 times the number. Find the number.

2. If a 56 in. board is cut into two parts such that the first part is 8 more than 3 times the second, find the length of each part.

3. The length of a rectangle is 10 more than twice its width. The perimeter is 50 cm. Find the length and the width.

Solve each equation. Round to the nearest hundredth where necessary.

4. $\frac{1}{3}x - \frac{1}{4} = \frac{3}{8}$

5. $0.21x + 0.4 = 0.009$

6. $\frac{5}{6} + \frac{2}{3}x = \frac{3}{4} - \frac{1}{2}x$

7. $1.14 - 0.45x = 1.2x + 0.37$

Answer each question.

8. 52 is 40% of what number?

9. What number is 26% of 185?

10. Joan got a $.75 raise this year. Last year she was paid $8 an hour. What was Joan's percent of increase?

11. A store sells a bike for $67.50. The profit is 35% of the cost. Find the cost of the bike.

Name _____   Date _____

Solve each equation for *x*. Round to the nearest hundredth where necessary.

1. $\frac{2}{3}x - \frac{1}{7} = \frac{1}{6}$

2. $\frac{3x}{5} + \frac{2x-1}{10} = \frac{3}{4} - \frac{x}{2}$

3. $0.78x - 3.1 = 4.952$

4. $1.6 + 2.142x = 0.18x - 2.15$

Solve each equation.

5. A 60-inch piece of string is cut into two pieces. The first piece is 6 inches longer than twice the second piece. Find the length of each piece.

6. The base of an isosceles triangle is 5 m less than 4 times the length of a side. The perimeter is 67 m. Find the length of each side and the base.

7. The width of a rectangle is 12 ft. more than twice its length. The perimeter is 90 ft. Find the length and the width.

8. What number is 15% of 48?

9. 112 is what percent of 560?

10. The cost of a concert ticket decreased from $20 to $17.50. Find the percent of decrease.

11. Matt bought a stereo for $700. The store made a profit of 40%. What was the cost of the stereo?

12. Trish earns $375 a week plus a 14% interest on her sales. She earned $1,145 last week. What were her sales?

Solving inequalities using addition and subtraction

An inequality contains two expressions with an inequality symbol, such as $<$, $>$, $\leq$, $\geq$, or $\neq$. Solve an inequality, just like an equation, by finding its solution set.

$x - 6 > 4$	Solve for x.
$x - 6 + 6 > 4 + 6$	Add 6 to both sides of inequality sign.
$x > 10$	The solution set is all values greater than 10.

The graph of this solution is:

$2x + 7 \leq x + 13$	Solve for x.
$2x - x + 7 - 7 \leq x - x + 13 - 7$	Subtract x and 7 from both sides.
$x \leq 6$	The solution set is all values less than or equal to 6.

The graph of this solution is:

Note: In the above examples, an open circle is at the point 10 because $x > 10$, is not equal to 10, and a closed circle is at point 6 because x is less than or equal to 6, so the point 6 needs to be included.

Graph each solution set below.

1. $x < -3$ **2.** $x \leq 2$ **3.** $x < 9$

4. $x \geq 5$ **5.** $x > -1$ **6.** $x > 4$

Solve each inequality. Graph the solution set.

7. $x + 9 > 10$ **8.** $-2 \geq x + 5$ **9.** $4x - (3 + 3x) > -2$

10. $x - 8 < 3$ **11.** $3 \leq x - 3$ **12.** $-5x + 2 + 6x < 3$

Write the inequality for each problem. Solve each problem.

13. If Dan gains 5 yards, he will rush more than 150 yards in today's game. How many yards has Dan already rushed.

14. After Tara gave 2 dozen cookies away, she still had more than 50 cookies. How many cookies did Tara have before she gave 2 dozen away?

Name _____ Date _____

Solving inequalities using multiplication and division

To solve inequalities, multiplication and division are often needed. This works much like solving an equation. However, there is one difference to point out. When multiplying or dividing by a negative number in an inequality, reverse the original inequality sign to its opposite to make the new inequality true.

$12 - 8x < 76$ Solve for x.

$12 - 12 - 8x < 76 - 12$ Subtract 12 from both sides of the inequality.

$\frac{-8x}{-8} < \frac{64}{-8}$ Divide both sides by -8.

$x > -8$ Reverse the original inequality since a negative number was used when dividing.

Thus, the solution is all values greater than -8. The graph is: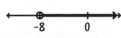

Solve each inequality.

1. $\frac{1}{3}x > 5$

2. $2x < -12$

3. $4x \leq 12$

4. $-3x \leq 9$

5. $-\frac{1}{4}x \geq 3$

6. $-2x > -14$

7. $\frac{2}{5}x \geq -8$

8. $-5x < 0$

9. $\frac{1}{5}x \leq -6$

Solve each inequality. Graph each solution set.

10. $-3 + 2x < 5$

11. $6 + 5x \leq -9$

12. $-7x + 2 < 6 - 5x$

13. $4 - 3x \geq -8$

14. $-12 > 8 + 4x$

15. $4 + 9x \geq 5x - 12$

Write an inequality for each problem. Solve the problem.

16. Jane, Sherri, and Katie collected more than 132 seashells. They each collected the same amount. How many did each girl collect?

17. Mary paid less than $3.50 for a package of 10 candy bars. What was the cost of each candy bar?

Solving compound inequalities

Compound inequalities contain two or more inequalities to be solved and graphed on the same number line. Often, a compound inequality needs to be solved first in order to be able to graph its solution.

$-4 \le 2x - 2 \le 6$	Solve for x.
$-4 + 2 \le 2x - 2 + 2 < 6 + 2$	Add 2 to each expression.
$\frac{-2}{2} \le \frac{2x}{2} \le \frac{8}{2}$	Divide each expression by 2.
$-1 \le x \le 4$	

Thus, the solution set is all real numbers that are greater than or equal to -1 and less than or equal to 4.

$2x - 3 > 3$	or	$3x + 2 < 8$	Solve each inequality for x.
$2x - 3 + 3 > 3 + 3$		$3x + 2 - 2 < 8 - 2$
$2x > 6$		$3x < 6$
$x > 3$		$x < 2$

Thus, the solution set is all real numbers greater than 3 or less than 2.

Note: When solving an inequality like the first example, and needing to multiply/divide by a negative number, remember you must reverse both inequality signs.

Write a compound inequality to represent each situation.

1. Crystal wants to weigh more than 120 pounds but less than 135 pounds.

2. Jerry wants to save at least $250.

3. Cheryl takes no more than 3 children in the car with her.

4. The length of Ellie's ribbon should be at least 12 inches and at the most 18 inches.

Solve each compound inequality.

5. $-14 \le 2x - 4 \le 2$

6. $6x - 1 \ge 11$ or $x + 7 \le 3$

7. $3x + 3 < 9$ or $5x > 20$

8. $7 \le 3x + 1 \le 10$

9. $32 > 16 - 4x > 12$

10. $-8x + 7 > -9$ and $-x - 2 < 5$

Graphing compound inequalities

To graph compound inequalities, solve the inequalities (if needed) and
graph each solution set on the same number line.

Graph $3 < x \le 9$

This solution is all real numbers greater than 3 and less than or equal to 9. The graph is:

Graph $x > 5$ or $x < -2$

This solution is all real numbers greater than 5 <u>or</u> less than -2. The graph is:

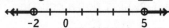

note: When the solution is similar to the first example, the graph will be *between* two values
on the number line. When the solution is similar to the second example, the graph will go in
opposite directions on the number line.

Match each inequality with its graph. Write the letter of the graph next to its problem number.

1. $x \ge -3$ or $x < 2$

a.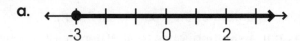

2. $x \le -3$ or $x > 2$

b.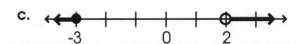

3. $x \le -3$ and $x > 2$

c.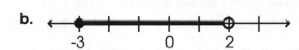

4. $x \ge -3$ or $x > 2$

d.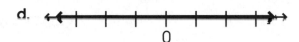

5. $x \ge -3$ and $x < 2$

e. ←——|——|——|——|——|——|——|——→
                    0

Graph each solution set.

6. $x > 5$ or $x < -6$

7. $4x > 8$ or $x - 2 < 1$

8. $-4 \le x < 3$

9. $-3x > 9$ or $2x - 6 > 8$

10. $x \le 3$ or $x > 4$

11. $6 > -4 - x > -2$

Graphing linear inequalities with two variables

A linear inequality can be written in the following forms:

$$ax + by < c \qquad ax + by \leq c \qquad ax + by > c \qquad ax + by \geq c$$

where (x, y) is an ordered pair that is a solution of the linear inequality, making the inequality true.

> Is $(-2, 5)$ a solution of $2x - 6y > 12$?
>
> $2(-2) - 6(5) > 12$ Substitute the x and y values into the inequality.
>
> $-4 - 30 > 12$
>
> $-34 > 12$ Not true. Therefore, $(-2, 5)$ is not a solution.

To sketch a graph of a linear inequality, follow these simple steps.

1. Sketch the graph of the corresponding linear equation using a dashed line for ‹ or › and a solid line for ≤ or ≥. Thus, separating the coordinate plane into two half planes.

2. Pick a point in each of the half planes and test each to find which one is a solution to the linear inequality.

3. Shade the half of the plane that contains the point that is a solution to the linear inequality.

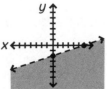

The graph of the above example of $2x - 6y > 12$ is shown.

Note: Since $(-2, 5)$ was not a solution, choose another point on the other half of the plane to show what half needs to be shaded.

Write **yes** or **no** to state whether the given point is a solution of the inequality.

1. $2x - 3y \leq 7$; $(5, -4)$

2. $-x - y > 5$; $(-2, -4)$

3. $5x + 4y \geq 8$; $(-2, 6)$

4. $-7x + 8y < 12$; $(-3, 2)$

Sketch the graph of each inequality.

5. $x + y < 5$

6. $x > -1$

7. $2x - y \geq 2$

8. $y \leq 3$

9. $-3x + 4y \leq 12$

10. $5x - 2y > -10$

Name _____   Date _____

Graphing equations with absolute values

The absolute value of a real number is the distance between that number and zero on a number line. To graph the equation $y = a|x + b| + c$, follow these steps.

1. Set $x + b = 0$ and solve for x. The result is the x-coordinate of the vertex. The vertex of the graph of an absolute value equation is the lowest point for a graph that opens up and the highest point for one that opens down.

2. Choose several values of x using the x-coordinate of the vertex, making sure you have some values to its right and some to its left. Solve for y, placing these points in a table.

3. Plot the points in the table and draw the v-shaped graph. (Remember: In the equation $y = a|x + b| + c$, if a is positive, the graph will open up, and if a is negative, the graph will open down.)

Graph $y = -3|x + 2| - 6$

$x + 2 = 0$

$x = -2$

Solve for x, the x-coordinate of the vertex.
The result is the x-coordinate of the vertex.
Make a table of x-values to the right and left of -2.

x	-4	-2	0
$y = -3|x + 2| - 6$	-12	-6	-12

Plot the points, making a v-shaped graph.
note: the vertex is (-2, -6), and the graph is going to open down, since $a = -3$.

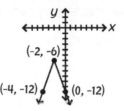

Find each vertex point.

1. $y = -2|x| + 5$

2. $y = 4|x - 3|$

3. $y = |x + 1| - 2$

4. $y = |x + 2| - 2$

5. $y = -|x| - 4$

6. $y = -3|x - 5| + 7$

Sketch the graph of each equation.

7. $y = 3|x|$

8. $y = 4|x + 5| - 2$

9. $y = -7|x|$

10. $y = -2|x - 1| + 4$

11. $y = |x + 6|$

12. $y = 5|x + 2| - 1$

Name _____   Date _____

Solving equations with absolute values

Remember, the absolute value of a real number is the distance between that number and 0 on a number line. For example, 7 and -7 both have an absolute value of 7 since they are both the same distance from 0, 7 units. Therefore, we can write the equation $|x| = 7$ as $x = 7$ or $x = -7$. Thus, this equation has two solutions, 7 and -7.

So, when solving absolute value equations, simply set the expression, within the absolute value sign, equal to a negative and to a positive and solve for x in both.

$|x + 4| = 5$	$-9 + 2|x - 5| = 11$ Add 9 to both sides.
$x + 4 = 5$ or $x + 4 = -5$	$2|x - 5| = 20$ Divide by 2 on both sides.
$x = 1$ $x = -9$	$|x - 5| = 10$
Thus, the solutions are 1 and -9.	$x - 5 = 10$ or $x - 5 = -10$
	$x = 15$ $x = -5$
	Thus, the solutions are 15 and -5.

Note: First, get the absolute value by itself before setting the expression within it equal to a negative and a positive number.

Isolate each absolute value on one side of the equation.

1. $6 + |8x - 3| = 12$

2. $9 + 3|x + 2| = 12$

3. $|x - 16| - 11 = 13$

4. $-4|x - 6| - 5 = 15$

Solve each equation.

5. $|x| = 6$

6. $|8 - x| = 5$

7. $-8 + 5|2x - 1| = 17$

8. $-3|x| = -27$

9. $3|x + 12| = 15$

10. $4|3x - 3| + 10 = 34$

11. $|x + 5| = 12$

12. $-2|x - 1| = -4$

13. $|x - 2| = 7$

14. $-7 + |x + 8| = 9$

Solving inequalities with absolute values

When solving inequalities with an absolute value, remember the following:

1. $|ax + b| < c$, where a, b, and c are real numbers, is equal to $-c < ax + b < c$.
   ($<$ can be replaced with $\leq$.)
2. $|ax + b| > c$, where a, b, and c are real numbers, is equal to $ax + b < -c$ or $ax + b > c$.
   ($>$ can be replaced with $\geq$.)

Once the absolute value inequality is set up as one of the above compound inequalities, solve for the values of x.

$|x + 7| < 10$

$-10 < x + 7 < 10$

$-17 < x < 3$

Thus, the solution is all real numbers greater than -17 and less than 3.

$|x - 12| \geq 13$

$x - 12 \leq -13$ or $x - 12 \geq 13$

$x \leq -1$ $x \geq 25$

Thus, the solution is all real numbers less than -1 or greater than 25.

Rewrite each absolute value as a compound inequality.

1. $|x| > 7$

2. $|x| \leq 2$

3. $|7 - 3x| > 10$

4. $|x - 9| < 12$

5. $|2x - 5| \geq /$

6. $|5 + 6x| < 11$

Solve each inequality.

7. $|x - 3| < 6$

8. $|3 - x| \leq 5$

9. $|2x + 1| \leq 7$

10. $|7 + x| \geq 8$

11. $|3x - 3| > 12$

12. $|8 - x| < 3$

Solve each inequality. Sketch its graph.

13. $|x + 9| < 1$

14. $|1 + 2x| > 5$

15. $|x + 7| > 6$

16. $|4x - 10| \geq 2$

17. $|6 - x| \leq 3$

18. $|3x - 6| \leq 12$

Problem solving using inequalities

When solving word problems with inequalities, the following translations
may be helpful.

1. $x < a$ (x is less than a.)
2. $x > a$ (x is greater than a.)
3. $x \geq a$ (x is greater than or equal to a, x is at least a, x is not less than a.)
4. $x \leq a$ (x is less than or equal to a, x is at most a, x is not greater than a.)
5. $a < x < b$ (x is between a and b, but b has to be greater than a.)

The Jones rented a boat for the day for $50 a day plus $10 for every hour they have the
boat. How long can they have the boat if they want to spend at the most $140?

$50 + 10h \leq 140$ Set up the equation, letting h = the number of hours.

$10h \leq 90$

$h \leq 9$ Therefore, they can have the boat at the most 9 hours that day.

Translate each sentence into an inequality.

1. Six more than 12 times a number is at the most 45.

2. The sum of 4 and a number multiplied by 8 is at least 20.

3. Seven less than 5 times a number is greater than 25.

4. A third of Joe's age is between 18 and 30.

Write an inequality for each problem. Solve.

5. Mike rented a bike for $10 a day plus $.25 a mile. How far can Mike ride his bike if he only wants to spend $25?

6. The sum of two consecutive odd integers is at least 36. Find the integers.

7. Steve makes a $15 profit on each stereo he sells. How many stereos does Steve need to sell to make a profit of at least $300?

8. Bob can lift 75 pounds. If a single brick weighs $2\frac{1}{2}$ pounds at most, how many bricks could Bob lift?

Review of Unit 7

Topics covered:
Solving Inequalities Using Addition and Subtraction   Graphing Equations with Absolute Values
Solving Inequalities Using Multiplication and Division   Solving Equations with Absolute Values
Solving Compound Inequalities   Solving Inequalities with Absolute Values
Graphing Compound Inequalities   Problem Solving Using Inequalities
Graphing Linear Inequalities with Two Variables

Solve each inequality. Graph the solution set.

1. $4 \le x + 1$ **2.** $-3x > 15$ **3.** $\frac{1}{3}x \le 2$ **4.** $8 - 3x \le 7x - 12$

Solve each compound inequality. Graph the solution set.

5. $-8 < x + 4 < 6$ **6.** $6 \le 3x - 6 \le 12$

7. $2x - 3 > 5$ or $3x + 7 < 10$ **8.** $2 - 5x \ge 7$ or $x + 1 \le -4$

Write **yes** or **no** to state whether the given point is a solution of the inequality.

9. $x - y \le 5$; (3, -1)   **10.** $3x - 5y > -10$; (-2, 5)

Find each vertex point.

11. $y = -2|x - 5| + 7$ **12.** $y = -|x| + 10$ **13.** $y = 5|x + 4| - 6$

Sketch each graph.

14. $-5x + 6y \le 30$ **15.** $y = 5|x + 2| - 1$ **16.** $2x - y > 3$

Solve.

17. $|x + 9| = 12$ **18.** $4|2x - 6| = 16$ **19.** $|4x - 4| \ge 12$ **20.** $|2x - 1| < 7$

Write an inequality. Solve.

21. John rented a van for $250 for the week plus $.20 a mile. How far can John drive if he only wants to spend a total of $325?

Unit 7 Test

Solve each problem. Graph its solution set.

1. $2x + 4 < -2$

2. $4x + 6 > 7x - 3$

3. $\frac{1}{4}x \geq -3$

4. $-3x \geq 15$

5. $4x + 1 > -3$ or $-\frac{2}{3}x < 2$

6. $-8 + 3x \geq 13$ or $6 + x \leq 7$

7. $-5 \leq x + 3 \leq 6$

8. $7 < 2x + 1 < 13$

9. $5x + 6 \geq -(3x + 10)$

Circle the point that is a solution of the inequality.

10. $2x - 4y > 10$; (3, -2), (4, 1)

11. $-x - y \leq 2$; (-2, -2), (-1, 2)

Find each vertex point. Graph.

12. $y = |x + 2| - 6$

13. $y = -2|x - 3| + 4$

14. $y = -|x| + 3$

15. $y = 7|x + 2|$

Sketch each graph.

16. $4x + 7y < -28$

17. $3x - y > 6$

18. $-5x + 4y \geq 20$

Solve.

19. $|x + 2| = 5$

20. $6|3x - 3| = 54$

21. $|2x + 4| \leq 6$

22. $3 + 5|x - 1| \geq 18$

Write an inequality. Solve.

23. The sum of three consecutive even integers is at the most 66. Find the three integers.

Name _____   Date _____

Solving linear systems by graphing

A linear system is a set of two or more equations including two or more variables. Each equation in a linear system contains a solution set of ordered pairs. The ordered pair that makes each of the linear equations in the system true is the solution of the system.

Is (3, 2) the solution to the system: $x - 2y = -1$ Check: $3 - 2(2) = -1$ true
                                          $-3x + 4y = -1$ $-3(3) + 4(2) = -1$ true

Thus (3, 2) is the solution of the system.

To solve a system like this one, simply graph each of the equations on the same coordinate plane and find the point at which the two lines intersect. The point of intersection is the solution of the system.

Graph the above system of equations and see if they indeed intersect at the point (3, 2).

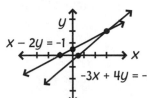

The point (3, 2) does appear to be the solution of this system since the two lines intersected at this point.

Tell whether the given ordered pair is a solution of the system. State **yes** or **no**.

1. $y = 2x - 3$;   (-2, -7)
    $y - 4x + 1$

2. $3x - 5y = 12$;   (5, 1)
    $x + 2y = 3$

3. $x + 2y = -4$;   (0, -2)
    $-x - 3y = 6$

Solve each system by graphing.

4. $4x + 3y = 6$
    $x - 4y = 11$

5. $x - y = 3$
    $2x - y = 5$

6. $y = 4x - 3$
    $y = -x - 8$

7. $y = 2x + 2$
    $y = 5x - 1$

8. $y = 3$
    $y = x - 5$

9. $y = -5x + 5$
    $y = -x - 3$

10. $x = -4$
    $y = -3x - 5$

11. $2x - 4y = -8$
    $-5x + 3y = -1$

12. $y = \frac{1}{2}x$
    $3y = x - 1$

Solving linear systems using the substitution method

Another method used to solve linear systems is called the substitution method.
Follow these four steps when using this method.

1. Solve one of the equations for one of its variables.
2. Substitute the expression found in step 1 into the other equation and solve for the other variable.
3. Substitute the value found in step 2 into the expression found in step 1 and solve.
4. Check the solution in each of the original equations.

Solve $\quad x - y = 2$

$\quad\quad\quad 2x + 3y = -6$

1. $x = y + 2$ Solve for x.
2. $2(y + 2) + 3y = -6$ Substitute $y + 2$ for x.
  $2y + 4 + 3y = -6$ Solve for y.
  $5y = -10$
3. $y = -2$ Substitute y-value into $x = y + 2$.
  So, $x = 0$.

Check $\quad 0 - (-2) = 2 \quad 2(0) + 3(-2) = -6$

$\quad\quad\quad\quad 2 = 2 \quad\quad\quad\quad -6 = -6$

$\quad\quad\quad\quad$ true $\quad\quad\quad\quad\quad$ true

Thus, the solution of this system is $(0, -2)$.

Solve one of the equations for one of its variables.

1. $3x + y = 4$
$\quad -2x - 5y = 7$

2. $x - 5y = 10$
$\quad 4x + 2y = 9$

3. $-7x + 3y = 14$
$\quad 6x + y = -3$

4. $8x - 5y = -10$
$\quad -x - 5y = 11$

Solve each system using the substitution method.

5. $y = x$
$\quad 4x - 3y = -1$

6. $5x - y = -5$
$\quad x - y = 3$

7. $2x + y = -11$
$\quad x + 2y = -1$

8. $x = 3y + 10$
$\quad -2x - 5y = 2$

9. $3y - 4 + x = 0$
$\quad 5x + 6y = 11$

10. $8x + 5y = 7$
$\quad -x - y = 1$

11. $y = x + 3$
$\quad x + 2y = -3$

12. $x + 2y = 2$
$\quad 7x + 10y = 2$

13. $2x - y = 5$
$\quad x - 3y = 0$

Solving linear systems using addition

To solve a linear system using addition, follow these four steps.

1. Arrange the equations with like terms in columns. Note that to use this method, the same variable must have opposite coefficients in the two equations.
2. Add the equations and solve for the variable that remains.
3. Substitute the value found in step 2 into either of the original equations and solve for other variable.
4. Check the solution in each of the original equations.

Solve the system	$-x + 2y = 5$	Note the $-x$ in one equation and the $+x$ in the other.
	$\underline{+\ x - 4y = -1}$	Add both equations.
	$-2y = 4$	Solve for y because y is remaining variable.
	$y = -2$	
	$-x + 2(-2) = 5$	Substitute the y-value into an original equation.
	$x = -9$	Solve for x.

Check $-(-9) + 2(-2) = 5$ $-9 - 4(-2) = -1$ Substitute the values into both original equations.

$9 + (-4) = 5$ $-9 + 8 = -1$

$5 = 5$ $-1 = -1$ Both are true.

Thus, the solution of this system is $(-9, -2)$.

Solve each system using addition.

1. $x - 2y = 2$
$x + 2y = 4$

2. $5x - 4y = 1$
$7x + 4y = 11$

3. $-5x + y = 8$
$5x - 2y = 2$

4. $-2x + 12y = 15$
$2x + y = 11$

5. $-3x + 4y = 15$
$3x + 6y = 5$

6. $-x + 2y = 8$
$x + 6y = 16$

7. $3x - y = 11$
$x + y = -3$

8. $y = -x + 3$
$y = x + 5$

9. $2x - 7y = 3$
$3x + 7y = 2$

10. $4x - y = 12$
$y - 3x = -6$

11. $x + 3y = 7$
$-3y = 2x - 5$

12. $y = -6x + 4$
$-6x + y = 12$

13. Explain why you cannot solve the following system simply by adding. Tell what you can do to the first equation so you can solve by adding.

$x - 5y = 7$

$3x + 4y = 11$

Name _____   Date _____

Solving linear systems using multiplication and addition

To solve a linear system using both multiplication and addition, use the following steps:

1. Arrange the equations with like terms in columns.
2. Look at the coefficients of x and y in both equations. Multiply one or both equations by a specific number that gives new coefficients for x (or y) that are opposites.
3. Add the equations and solve for the variable that remains.
4. Substitute the value found in step 3 into one of the original equations and solve for the other variable.
5. Check the solution in both of the original equations.

Solve $3x - y = 2$ $4(3x - y) = 4(2)$ $12x - 4y = 8$ Multiply the first equation by 4.

$-2x + 4y = 2$ $\underline{+ \ -2x + 4y = 2}$ Add.

$10x = 10$ Solve for x, the remaining variable.

$x = 1$

Substitute the x-value into one of original equations and solve for y. $3(1) - y = 2$

Check $3(1) - 1 = 2$ $-2(1) + 4(1) = 2$ $3 - y = 2$

$3 - 1 = 2$ $-2 + 4 = 2$ $y = 1$

$2 = 2$ True $2 = 2$ True

Thus, the solution of the linear system is $(1, 1)$.

State the best number to be multiplied by one equation to eliminate one of the variables using addition.

1. $x - 2y = 4$
$-3x + 5y = -3$

2. $-3x - 6y = 11$
$2x + y = 4$

3. $7x + 2y = 5$
$-x - 6y = 8$

4. $6x - 5y = 8$
$-2x - y = 3$

Solve each system using multiplication and addition.

5. $4x + y = 5$
$2x + 5y = 7$

6. $7x + 2y = -4$
$3x + 6y = 24$

7. $-2x + 5y = 8$
$-5x + 3y = 1$

8. $-5x + 2y = 22$
$-3x + 2y = 6$

9. $x + y = 0$
$2x - 11y = 39$

10. $-3x + 4y = 1$
$x + 2y = 3$

11. $2x + 3y = 12$
$5x + 2y = 8$

                                         Algebra

Recognizing special types of linear systems

Solving Systems of Linear Equations

A system of linear equations can have one solution, many solutions, or no solutions. A system that has one solution is going to be two lines that intersect. A system that has infinitely many solutions is actually the same line. A system that has no solutions is a system that contains parallel lines.

Solve $\quad -x + y = 2 \quad$ Add equations.
$\qquad\quad x - y = 3$
$\qquad\qquad\quad 0 = 5$

Shows no solution because $0 = 5$ does not make sense. Look at its graph below. Graphs into two parallel lines.

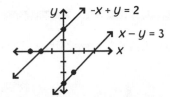

Solve $\quad 3x - y = 2 \quad$ Multiply by 2. $\quad 6x - 2y = 4$
$\qquad\quad 6x - 2y = 4 \quad$ Multiply by -1. $\quad -6x + -2y = -4$
$\qquad\qquad\qquad\qquad$ Add equations. $\qquad\qquad 0 = 0$

Shows infinitely many solutions. Look at its graph below. Graphs into the same line.

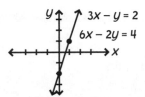

Write the letter of the graph beside the problem number with the matching system. Describe each graph's solution.

a.

b.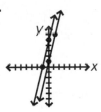

c.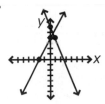

d.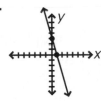

1. $y = 3x - 2$
$\quad 3x + y = 5$

2. $-2x + y = 4$
$\quad 2x + y = 6$

3. $4x + 2y - 6$
$\quad y = -2x + 3$

4. $5x - y - -5$
$\quad y = 5x + 1$

Graph each system and describe its solutions.

5. $3x - 2y = 4$
$\quad -6x + 4y = 8$

6. $y = -5x + 1$
$\quad x + y = -3$

7. $-7x + 8y = 12$
$\quad 7x - 8y = 4$

8. $x - y = 3$
$\quad x - y = 2$

9. $x + 3y = 7$
$\quad 3x + 9y = 21$

10. $x + y = 3$
$\quad 2x + 2y = 6$

11. $y = 2x - 3$
$\quad -4x + 2y = -6$

12. $4x - 5y = -4$
$\quad -2x + y = -4$

13. $y = \frac{2}{3}x + 1$
$\quad x + 2y = 9$

Name _____   Date _____

Solving systems of linear inequalities

A system of linear inequalities consists of two or more inequalities with two or more variables. The solution of an inequality system is an ordered pair that is a solution of each inequality in the system. The graph of a system shows all solutions of the system.

Solve $y \geq x - 2$ by graphing.

$2x - y \leq 6$

Graph both lines.

Shade each line's half plane.

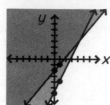

Thus, the solution of the linear inequality is the double-shaded region, containing all the points that are solutions of the system.

State whether each inequality would be a **solid** or a **dashed** line. Tell whether you would shade **above** or **below** the line.

1. $3x - y \leq 7$

2. $6x - y < 10$

3. $y \leq 2x - 8$

4. $4x + 5y > 2$

5. $x + y \geq -5$

6. $y < 9x + 1$

Solve each linear inequality system by graphing.

7. $x \geq 2$

$y \leq 4$

8. $y \geq 3x + 1$

$y \leq -x - 4$

9. $4x - 5y < -20$

$3x + 2y \geq 6$

10. $x \geq -3$

$y \geq 4$

$x < 2$

11. $y \leq -3$

$y > 5$

12. $y < 5x + 2$

$y > -2x - 3$

13. $y - x < 0$

$2x - y > -3$

14. $y \leq 0$

$x + y \leq 5$

$y \geq -x + 2$

Problem solving using linear systems

Solving Systems of Linear Equations

Linear systems are often needed to solve more complex word problems. These can involve digits, age, money, and many more real world subjects.

> Sherri is twice as old as Harry. In 10 years, she will be 15 years older than Harry. How old are both Sherri and Harry now?

To solve, let s = Sherri's age now, $s + 10$ = Sherri's age in 10 years,
let h = Harry's age now, $h + 10$ = Harry's age in 10 years.

Write two equations: $s = 2h$
                           $s + 10 = h + 15$

Solve the system $2h + 10 = h + 15$ Substitute $2h$ in for s.
                      $h = 5$ Solve for h.
                      $s = 2(5)$ Substitute 5 in for h in original equation.
                      $s = 10$

Check $10 = 2(5)$ $10 + 10 = 5 + 15$
         $10 = 10$ True $20 = 20$ True

Thus, Sherri is 10 years old, and Harry is 5 years old.

Use linear systems to solve each problem.

1. Cheryl is 4 times as old as Josh. In 6 years, she will be 12 years older than Josh. What is each person's age today?

2. The sum of two numbers is 50. Their difference is 6. Find the numbers.

3. If Joe and Jim combined their hourly pay, they would have $16. Jim's hourly pay is $1.50 more than Joe's. Find each boy's hourly pay.

4. At a restaurant, one hamburger and two orders of fries costs $2.50. Two hamburgers and three orders of fries costs $4.25. At this rate, find the cost of one hamburger and one order of fries.

5. Molly has a collection of coins worth $5.20. She has 8 more nickels than quarters. How many nickels and quarters does Molly have?

Review of Unit 8

Topics covered:

Solving Linear Systems by Graphing	Recognizing Special Types of Linear Systems
Solving Linear Systems Using the Substitution Method	Solving Systems of Linear Inequalities
Solving Linear Systems Using Addition	Problem Solving Using Linear Systems
Solving Linear Systems Using Multiplication and Addition	

Circle the point that is the solution of each linear system.

1. $-2x + 5y = 9$ $(-2, 1)$
   $-x + 3y = 5$ $(2, 3)$

2. $6x - 3y = -15$ $(5, -5)$
   $5x - 4y = -5$ $(-5, -5)$

Solve each system by graphing and describe its solutions.

3. $x - y = 4$
   $y = x - 2$

4. $-2x + y = 4$
   $2x + y = 6$

5. $y \leq -x - 2$
   $3x - y \geq 5$

6. $3x + 4y = 12$
   $y = -\frac{3}{4}x + 3$

7. $y \geq 1$
   $x < 3$

8. $y > 3$
   $y < -3$

Solve each system using the substitution method.

9. $7x - y = 9$
   $2x - 2y = -6$

10. $y = 4x - 5$
   $5x - 6y = 11$

Solve each system using multiplication and addition.

11. $x - y = 2$
   $2x + 3y = 4$

12. $-3x + 10y = 2$
   $-2x + 5y = 3$

Solve the following problem using a linear system.

13. When Joey mowed lawns for 10 hours and walked dogs for 4 hours, he made a total of $62. When he walked dogs for 5 hours and mowed the lawn for 8 hours, he made a total of $55. How much does Joey charge per hour for each job?

Unit 8 Test

1. Is (2, -3) a solution of this system? $-3x + y = -9$
   Explain why or why not. $4x - 2y = 14$

Choose the method that can be used to solve each of the systems below. Solve each system and state why you used the method you used. Be sure to use each method at least once.

2. $x = 2y + 3$
   $3x - 2y = 1$

3. $2x - y = 12$
   $-2x + 3y = -4$

4. $y = x$
   $6x - 5y = -4$

5. $y = -4x + 5$
   $y = -5x + 8$

6. $y = -6x + 1$
   $4x - 2y = -2$

7. $3x - y = 2$
   $2x + 2y = 12$

Describe each of the following solutions. If there is one solution, state the solution.

8. $y = 2x + 6$
   $2x - y = 3$

9. $x + 2y = 4$
   $-x + 6y = 12$

10. $x = 2y - 7$
    $8x + 5y = 7$

11. $4x - 5y - 12$
    $5y = 4x - 12$

12. $y = -7x + 3$
    $21x + 3y = 9$

13. $6x - y = 4$
    $-12x + 2y = 8$

Solve each system by graphing.

14. $x > 3$
    $2x + 4y \geq 12$

15. $y \leq -2$
    $x > -4$
    $y \leq -4x - 1$

16. $3x - 2y \geq 6$
    $y \leq 5x - 2$
    $y > 0$

Solve the following problem using a linear system.

17. Mike's age is 3 times John's age. In 12 years, Mike will be twice as old as John. How old are Mike and John now?

Multiplication properties of exponents

Working with Powers, Exponents, and Polynomials

When multiplying exponents, it is important to remember the following properties:

1. When multiplying powers having the same base, add the exponents, keeping the same base. (Remember: a^3, a is the base, 3 is the exponent, and a^3 is the power.) For example, $x^3 \cdot x^5 = x^{3+5} = x^8$.

2. When finding a power of a power, multiply the exponents. For example, $(x^3)^2 = x^6$.

3. When finding the power of a product, find the power of each factor and multiply. For example, $(x \cdot y)^2 = x^2 \cdot y^2$.

Simplify $(5x^3)^2(xy)^3$
$(5^2x^6)(x^3y^3)$
$= 25x^9y^3$

Simplify $(2x^4)^3(-x^2)^3$
$(2^3x^{12})(-x^6)$
$= -8x^{18}$

1. What do you do with the exponents when multiplying powers that have the same base?

2. Label the base, the exponent, and the power in x^3.

3. Explain what you are to do when finding the power of a product.

Simplify each expression.

4. $3x \cdot x^2$

5. $(-6xy)^2(x^2y)^3$

6. $(4z^4)^2(2x^2y)(-3xy^3z^5)$

7. $-4x^4 \cdot x^3$

8. $(4x^3y^2)^3(-2x^2y^4)$

9. $(3x)^2(2x^3y^6)(-5x^6y^2)$

10. $(-x^2)(-x)^2$

11. $-xy(-xy)^2$

12. $(3x^3)(5x^5)$

13. $(-2x^3y^3z)^4(2xyz^4)^2$

negative and zero exponents

Given a nonzero number a and a positive integer n, the following definitions of negative exponents and zero exponents are stated.

1. For a negative exponent: the expression a^{-n} is the reciprocal of a^n.
   This is written: $a^{-n} = \frac{1}{a^n}$, where $a \neq 0$.
2. For a zero exponent: any nonzero number raised to the 0 power will have an answer of 1.
   This is written: $a^0 = 1$, where $a \neq 0$.

Evaluate 5^{-3}

$$= \frac{1}{5^3}$$

$$= \frac{1}{125}$$

Simplify by rewriting with positive exponents. $2x^{-3}y^2z^{-4}$

$$= 2 \cdot \frac{1}{x^3} \cdot y^2 \cdot \frac{1}{z^4}$$

$$= \frac{2y^2}{x^3z^4}$$

note: When rewriting expressions to positive exponent form, simply move the factors from the denominator to the numerator or vice versa leaving out the in-between step.

1. Any number raised to the zero power has what value?

Rewrite each expression with positive exponents.

2. x^{-8}

3. $\frac{1}{3x^{-2}}$

4. $(-3)^0 x^{-3}$

5. x^{-10}

6. $\frac{1}{5x^{-4}}$

7. $\frac{6}{x^{-2}}$

8. $6x^{-3}$

9. $x^{-3}y^4$

10. $\frac{1}{(2x)^{-3}}$

11. $4x^{-5}$

12. $4x^{-4}y^{-2}$

13. $(3x^{-2})^2$

Evaluate each expression.

14. 4^{-2}

15. $7^3 \cdot 7^{-3}$

16. $3 \cdot 3^{-1}$

17. $-5^0 \cdot \frac{1}{3^{-3}}$

18. $(6^2)^{-2}$

19. $(-2^{-3})^{-1}$

Division properties of exponents

When dividing exponents, it is important to remember the following properties:

1. When dividing powers that have the same base, subtract the exponents.

   For example, $\frac{x^4}{x^2} = x^{4-2} = x^2$, where x cannot be equal to 0.

2. When finding a power of a quotient, find the power of the numerator and the power of the denominator and divide.

   For example, $(\frac{x}{y})^3 = \frac{x^3}{y^3}$, where y cannot be equal to 0.

Simplify $\frac{6^8}{6^6}$

$= 6^{8-6}$

$= 6^2 = 36$

Simplify $(\frac{3}{4})^{-2}$

$= \frac{3^{-2}}{4^{-2}}$

$= \frac{4^2}{3^2} = \frac{16}{9}$

1. Explain what you do with the exponents when dividing powers that have the same base.

Evaluate each expression.

2. $\frac{5^6}{5^3}$ **3.** $\frac{(-3)^2}{3^2}$ **4.** $\frac{3^2}{3^{-4}}$ **5.** $\frac{5^4 \cdot 5}{5^7}$ **6.** $(\frac{3}{2})^3$

7. $\frac{7^3}{7}$ **8.** $\frac{4^8}{4^8}$ **9.** $\frac{6^4 \cdot 6^3}{6^5}$ **10.** $(\frac{4}{5})^2$ **11.** $(\frac{-3}{4})^{-2}$

Simplify each expression.

12. $(\frac{3}{x})^3$ **13.** $x^5 \cdot \frac{1}{x^7}$ **14.** $\frac{18x^4y^2}{-6x^2y^4} \cdot \frac{-3x^2y^2}{-y}$

15. $\frac{x^3}{x^5}$ **16.** $\frac{4x^4y^4}{4x^2y^2} \cdot \frac{4x^2y^4}{2xy}$ **17.** $\frac{7x^{-3}y^3}{x^2y^{-3}} \cdot \frac{(2x^3y)^{-2}}{x^2y^2}$

18. $x^4 \cdot \frac{1}{x^2}$ **19.** $\frac{6x^2y^4}{3y^2} \cdot \frac{7x^2y^{-4}}{x^4}$ **20.** $\frac{8x^{-2}y^4}{x^3y^{-3}} \cdot \frac{(4xy^2)^{-1}}{x^{-2}y^{-2}}$

Scientific notation

Scientific notation uses powers of 10 to write decimal numbers. Numbers written in scientific notation contain a number between 1 and 10 multiplied by a power of 10. For example, the number, 3.1×10^2, is in scientific notation.
The number 45×10^2 is not written in scientific notation.

1. Change 450 to scientific notation.

4.5×10^2 A number between 1 and 10 is needed. Move the decimal two places to get 4.5. Therefore, the power of 10 is 2, since we moved the decimal two places to get 4.5.

2. Rewrite 3.4×10^3 in decimal form.

3,400 Since there is a positive power of 3, move the decimal 3 places to the right. (Note: If the power is negative, move the decimal to the left.)

3. Multiply $(5.4 \times 10^3)(2.2 \times 10^5)$

$(5.4 \times 2.2)(10^3 \times 10^5)$ Regroup into decimals and powers of 10.

$(11.88)(10^8)$ Simplify by multiplying decimals and adding powers.

$1.188 \times 10^{8+1}$ Add 1 to the 8 power since decimal moved 1 place.

1.188×10^9 Put in scientific notation.

Note: When multiplying, dividing, or finding the powers of numbers in scientific notation, simply use the properties of exponents.

Rewrite each scientific notation in decimal form.

1. 2.08×10^5

2. 4.5×10^3

3. 7.68×10^{-2}

4. 3.12×10^{-4}

5. 6.25×10^{-6}

6. 9.5765×10^4

Rewrite each decimal in scientific notation.

7. 68,000,000

8. 0.004953

9. 1,490,000,000,000

10. 9,000,000,000

11. 0.0975

12. 0.00000515

Evaluate each expression in scientific notation without using a calculator.

13. $(7 \times 10^{-3})(4 \times 10^5)$

14. $(5 \times 10^5)(3 \times 10^{-2})$

15. $(3 \times 10^{-4})(6 \times 10^2)$

16. $(6 \times 10^6)(6 \times 10^{-6})$

17. $(8 \times 10^{-5})(9 \times 10^{-3})$

18. $(7 \times 10^6)(5 \times 10^{-1})$

Simplifying polynomials

A monomial is an expression that can be a constant, a variable, or a product of a constant and one or more variables. A polynomial is a monomial or the sum of monomials. Specifically, a binomial is the sum of two monomials, and a trinomial is the sum of three monomials. Remember, like terms are terms that have the same variable(s) raised to the same power(s). A polynomial is considered to be in simplest form when there are no like terms. The degree of a term is the actual power of that term. A constant has a degree of 0. The degree of a polynomial is the largest degree of its terms.

1. Give the degree of the polynomial $3x^4 + 2x^2 - 1$.

    The degree is 4.   The largest degree of all three terms is 4.

2. Simplify $3x^5 + 4x - 2x^5 - 5x + 10$ and give its degree.

    $x^5 - x + 10$ Add like terms and put in simplest form.

    The degree is 5.   The greatest degree of all three terms is 5.

3. Simplify $4x^6 + 7x^4 - 8x^3 + 3x^3 - 9x^6 + x^4$ and put answer in standard form.

    $-5x^6 + 8x^4 - 5x^3$ Add like terms and put in simplest form.

    $8x^4 - 5x^6 - 5x^3$ Put terms in descending order, from largest degree to the smallest degree, which is standard form.

Give the definition of each term and give an example of each.

1. monomial   **2.** trinomial   **3.** standard form

4. binomial   **5.** degree   **6.** polynomial

Simplify each polynomial. Give the degree of the polynomial. Make sure each answer is in standard form.

7. $6x^3 - 4x^2 + 2x - 7x^3 + 5x$ **8.** $x^5 + 4x^2 - 7x^3 + 6x^2 - 2x^5 + 3x^3$

9. $10 - 7x^5 + 2x^4 - x^4 + 8x^5 - 3x^3$ **10.** $10x + 3x^2 - 8x + 6x^2$

11. $10x^4 - 7x^3 + 5x^3 - 4x^4 - 8x^4$ **12.** $-x^3 + 4x^2 - 7 + 3x^2 - 8x^3$

13. $4x^7 - 3x^5 + x^7 + 5x^5 + 4x^4 - 6$ **14.** $-6x + 5x^3 - 4x^2 + 3 + 9x^3 - 10x + 6x - 5$

Adding and subtracting polynomials

When adding polynomials, the following two methods can be used.

1. The horizontal method:

   Add $(3x^4 + 8x^2 - 2)$ and $(-4x^2 + 7x^4 + 5)$

   First group like terms in descending order. $(3x^4 + 7x^4) + (8x^2 - 4x^2) + (-2 + 5)$

   Simplify. $10x^4 + 4x^2 + 3$

2. The vertical method:

   Add $(4x^7 + 6x^4 - 10 + 2x^5)$ and $(10x^5 - 5x^7 - 3x^4 + 12)$

   Group like terms in columns in descending order.

$$4x^7 + 2x^5 + 6x^4 - 10$$
$$+\ -5x^7 + 10x^5 - 3x^4 + 12$$
$$\overline{-x^7 + 12x^5 + 3x^4 + 2}$$

   Simplify.

When subtracting polynomials, change the sign of each term in the second polynomial and then choose from one of the methods above to simplify.

Subtract. $(10x^7 - 4x^4 + 7x^2 + 2) - (12x^4 + 6x^7 + 8 - 5x^2)$

Change sign of each term in second polynomial. $10x^7 - 4x^4 + 7x^2 + 2 - 12x^4 - 6x^7 - 8 + 5x^2$

Choosing method 1 above, group like terms in descending order.

   $(10x^7 - 6x^7) + (-4x^4 - 12x^4) + (7x^2 + 5x^2) + (2 - 8)$

   Simplify. $4x^7 - 16x^4 + 12x^2 - 6$

---

1. What is important to remember to do when subtracting polynomials?

Simplify each problem by adding and subtracting.

2. $(7x - 5) - (3x + 7)$

3. $(2x^2 - 3x + 1) - (5x^2 - 3x + 10)$

4. $(6x + 7) + (8x - 3)$

5. $(x^3 - 7x^4 + 2x^2 - 3x) + (4x^4 - 8x^3 + 5x)$

6. $(9x^2 + 3x - 5) - (3x^2 + 4x - 10)$

7. $(8x^4 - 9x^3 + 2x) - (6x^4 + 7x^3 - 3x)$

8. $(6x^2 + 9x + 4) - (-7x^2 + 2x - 1)$

9. $(x^3 - x^2 + 2) - (x^3 + x^2 + 5)$

10. $(-8x^2 + 2) + (7x - 5)$

11. $(8x + 6) - (10x + 16) + (4x - 6)$

12. $(6x^2 + 7x - 9) + (3x + 8)$

13. $(4x^2 + 2) + (3x^2 - 4x + 6) - (5x^2 + 10)$

Multiplying polynomials by a monomial

To multiply a multi-termed polynomial by a monomial, simply multiply each term in the polynomial by the monomial using the distributive property. Remember the properties of exponents when simplifying such problems.

Multiply $3x(3x^3 - 2x^2 + 8x - 7)$

$3x(3x^3) - 3x(2x^2) + 3x(8x) - 3x(7)$ Distribute $3x$ to each term.

$9x^4 - 6x^3 + 24x^2 - 21x$ Multiply to simplify.

You may have to simplify an expression using the distributive property to multiply the polynomial by a monomial.

Simplify $4x^7 + 9x^4 - 7 + 2x^2(8x^5 - 5x^2)$

$4x^7 + 9x^4 - 7 + 2x^2(8x^5) - 2x^2(5x^2)$ Distribute the $2x$.

$4x^7 + 9x^4 - 7 + 16x^7 - 10x^4$ Multiply to begin simplifying.

$20x^7 - x^4 - 7$ Simplify.

Multiply each expression.

1. $6x(4x - 3)$

2. $4x(x^2 - 6x + 3)$

3. $(-3x^2 + 4x - 2)(-4x^3)$

4. $x(-5x + 2)$

5. $-3x(5x^2 - 2x - 6)$

6. $(-x^2 + 2x - 1)(5x^3)$

7. $-2x(-4x - 8)$

8. $-x^2(7x^2 - x + 4)$

9. $-5x^4(2x^2 - 8x + 6)$

Simplify each expression.

10. $-4x^2 - 5x + 7 + 3(x^2 + 8x - 2)$

11. $6x^2 + 3(x - 5) - 8x$

12. $5x^2 - 3x(x - 7)$

13. $2x^2 + 7x + 6 - 5x(-2x - 1)$

14. $6x^2 + 4x + (7x - 3)2x$

15. $-3x^2 - 3x(4x^2 - 5x + 7) - 8x^2$

16. $-x^2 + 8x - 6 - 7(3x^2 - 5x + 9)$

17. $x^3 + (7x^2 - 9x - 1)x + 10x^2$

Multiplying binomials

The easiest way to multiply binomials is to use what is called the FOIL method.
This method multiplies the first terms of the binomials (F), multiplies the outer terms
of the binomials (O), multiplies the inner terms of the binomials (I), multiplies the last
terms of the binomials (L), and simplifies by adding like terms.

1. Multiply $(3x - 2)(4x + 3)$

$3x(4x) = 12x^2$	Multiply first terms.	F
$3x(3) = 9x$	Multiply outer terms.	O
$-2(4x) = -8x$	Multiply inner terms.	I
$-2(3) = -6$	Multiply last terms.	L
$12x^2 + 9x - 8x - 6$	Simplify by combining like terms.	
$12x^2 + x - 6$	Final product	

2. Multiply $(5x + 2)(7x - 3)$

$$5x(7x) + 5x(-3) + 2(7x) + 2(-3)$$
$$\quad\; F \qquad\; O \qquad\;\; I \qquad\;\; L$$

$35x^2 - 15x + 14x - 6$	Multiply.
$35x^2 - x - 6$	Final product

Multiply.

1. $(x + 7)(x - 5)$

2. $(x - 5)(x - 5)$

3. $(9x - 1)(6x + 2)$

4. $(7x - 8)(8x - 7)$

5. $(x + 2)(x + 3)$

6. $(x + 7)(x - 7)$

7. $(3x + 5)(-4x - 7)$

8. $(-3x - 9)(-x - 6)$

9. $(x - 10)(x + 1)$

10. $(2x - 3)(5x + 4)$

11. $(-5x + 6)(x - 2)$

12. $(-4x + 4)(5x + 8)$

Simplify each expression.

13. $(3x^2 - 4y)(2x^2 + 5y)$

14. $(a^2 + b^2)(x^2 + y^2)$

15. $(4x^3 + 6x^2)(8x^3 - x^2)$

16. $(7x - 2)(x^2 + 3)$

17. $(a + b)(x + y)$

18. $(x^2 - 8)(x^2 + 5)$

Multiplying polynomials in two special cases

When multiplying polynomials, it is important to remember two special products.

1. Sum and difference product: $(a + b)(a - b) = a^2 - b^2$

Multiply	$(5x + 2)(5x - 2)$	$a = 5x, b = 2$
	$(5x)^2 - 2^2$	Square both terms.
	$25x^2 - 4$	The result is special product.

2. Square of a binomial product: $(a + b)^2 = a^2 + 2ab + b^2$
$$(a - b)^2 = a^2 - 2ab + b^2$$

Multiply	$(3x + 2)^2$	$a = 3x, b = 2$
	$(3x)^2 + 2(3x)(2) + 2^2$	Square a, square b, and multiply 2 times a and b.
	$9x^2 + 12x + 4$	The result is special product.
Multiply	$(4x - 5)^2$	$a = 4x, b = 5$
	$(4x)^2 - 2(4x)(5) + 5^2$	Square a, square b, and multiply 2 times a and b.
	$16x^2 - 40x + 25$	The result is special product.

Multiply each expression.

1. $(x - 8)^2$

2. $(2x + 4)^2$

3. $(x^2 + 3)^2$

4. $(3x - 2)(3x + 2)$

5. $(x - 6)^2$

6. $(x^2 - 4)^2$

7. $(x + 7)(x - 7)$

8. $(7x - y)(7x + y)$

9. $(4x + 1)(4x - 1)$

10. $(x - 9)(x + 9)$

11. $(8x - 2y)^2$

12. $(2 + 6x)(2 - 6x)$

Solve each equation for x.

13. $(x - 7)(x + 2) = (x - 4)^2$

14. $(x - 4)^2 = (x + 2)^2$

15. $(x - 8)^2 = x^2$

16. $(x + 5)^2 = (x + 5)(x - 5)$

17. $x^2 = (x + 10)^2$

18. $(x + 6)(x - 6) = (x + 6)^2$

Problem solving with compound interest

To find compound interest over a course of several years, use the formula:

$a = P(1 + r)^t$, where a is the balance, P is the principal, r is the annual interest rate, and t is the number of years.

Find the balance after 5 years if $1000 is deposited into an account that pays 5% annual interest compounded yearly.

$a = P(1 + r)^t$	Use the compound interest formula.
$a = 1000(1 + 0.05)^5$	Substitute the given values for each variable.
$a = 1000(1.05)^5$	Use a calculator to solve.
$a = \$1,276.28$	Round balance to the nearest cent.

Thus, the balance after 5 years is $1,276.28.

Solve each problem for its unknown. Round to the nearest cent.

1. A principal of $150 is deposited in an account that pays 8% interest compounded yearly. Find the balance of the account after 3 years.

2. How much should you deposit into an account that pays 6% interest compounded yearly to have a balance of $900 after 5 years?

3. $1,500 is deposited into an account that pays 6.5% interest compounded yearly. What is the balance after 4 years?

4. How much do you need to deposit into your account that pays 7% interest compounded yearly to have a balance of $2,500 after 8 years?

5. John's bonus this quarter was for $1,250. If he put it into an account that pays 8% interest compounded yearly, what would his balance be after 3 years? Is this more or less than a balance after 5 years if he put it into an account that pays 5% interest compounded yearly? What is the difference?

Review of Unit 9

Working with Powers, Exponents, and Polynomials

Topics covered:

Multiplication Properties of Exponents
Negative and Zero Exponents
Division Properties of Exponents
Scientific Notation
Simplifying Polynomials

Adding and Subtracting Polynomials
Multiplying Polynomials by a Monomial
Multiplying Binomials
Multiplying Polynomials in Two Special Cases
Problem Solving with Compound Interest

Simplify each expression using the properties of exponents. Use positive exponents only.

1. $(6x)x^5$

2. $(\frac{5}{4})^{-2}$

3. $\frac{x^6}{x^3}$

4. $8x^{-2}y^5z^{-3}$

5. $(3x^2y)(-8xy^4)$

6. $(-x^2y^4z^5)^6$

7. $\frac{-18x^{-2}y^2(x^4y^3)}{6x^5y^6}$

8. $\frac{(15x^{-2}y^{-4})^{-1}}{(30xy)^{-1}}$

9. Write 3.145×10^5 in decimal form.

10. Write 0.0000545 in scientific notation.

Add or subtract each problem. Give the degree of the polynomial. Make sure your answer is in standard form.

11. $(3x^3 - 4x + 3) + (-3x^3 + 5x - 8)$

12. $(-5x^5 + 7x^3 - 4x + 2) + (7x^5 - 8x^4 + 9x^3)$

13. $(4x^2 - 8x + 2) - (-5x^2 + 5x + 6)$

14. $(10x^3 - 8x^2 + 6x - 1) - (-7x^3 + 2x - 4)$

15. Explain how to use the FOIL method to multiply binomials.

Multiply each problem. Use special products where possible.

16. $2x(3x^3 - 7x^2 + 5x - 2)$

17. $(4x - 2)^2$

18. $(x^2 - 6y)(3x^2 + 4y)$

19. What is the balance after 5 years if you deposit $800 in an account that has 7% interest compounded yearly? Round your answer to the nearest cent.

Name _____   Date _____

1. Explain what you are to do when multiplying and dividing powers with the same base.

2. Define monomial, binomial, trinomial, and the degree of a polynomial, and give an example of each.

Simplify each expression using positive exponents.

3. $(5x^2y^3)(-3x^{-5}y^4)$

4. $-4x^5 \cdot 6x^{-5}$

5. $\dfrac{-20x^4y^{-5}z^3}{10x^{-5}y^{-3}z^7}$

6. $\dfrac{(3x^2y^4)^{-2}}{(4xy^2)(2x)}$

7. $-2x(-4x^2)^2$

8. $(-3x^{-2}y^5z^{-3})^{-2}$

9. Write 3.12×10^{-6} in decimal form.

10. Write 4,619,000,000,000 in scientific notation.

Add or subtract to simplify each polynomial. Give the degree of the polynomial. Make sure each answer is in standard form.

11. $(8x^4 - 8x^3 + 2) + (4x^4 - 5x + 7)$

12. $-5 + 9x^2 + 4x - 5x^2 + 2x^2 - 9x + 8x^3 - 6$

Multiply each expression.

13. $-3x^2(5x^2 - 6x + 2)$

14. $(7x - 2)^2$

15. $(-5x - y)(6x + 2y)$

16. Solve for x. $8 + x(x + 4) = (x - 2)^2$

17. What did you deposit if your balance after 3 years is $750 in an account that pays 6% interest compounded yearly?

Name _____   Date _____

Square roots

All positive real numbers have two square roots; one that is positive and one that is negative. A square root can be defined as follows:

If $b^2 = a$, then b would be the square root of a and $-b$ would be a square root of a.

The symbol $\sqrt{}$ means the principal square root of a number (the positive square root).

Find the square root of 36. Answers 6, –6 or ±6

$\sqrt{36}$ Answer: 6 $\pm\sqrt{\dfrac{9}{16}} = \pm\dfrac{3}{4}$

$-\sqrt{36}$ Answer: –6

In evaluating an expression containing square roots, use what is known about square roots.

Evaluate $\sqrt{b^2 - 4ac}$ for $a = 1$, $b = -6$, and $c = 5$.

$\sqrt{(-6)^2 - 4(1)(5)} = \sqrt{36 - 20} = \sqrt{16} = 4$

Note: The square root of a negative number is undefined so it has no square root. The square root of 0 is 0.

Find all the square roots of each number.

1. 81

2. 0

3. $\dfrac{9}{16}$

4. 0.25

5. 121

6. $\dfrac{36}{25}$

7. -16

8. 0.49

Evaluate each expression. Round to 2 decimal places when necessary.

9. $-\sqrt{196}$

10. $\sqrt{0.04}$

11. $-\sqrt{\dfrac{25}{144}}$

12. $-\sqrt{6.25}$

13. $\sqrt{45}$

14. $-\sqrt{121}$

15. $\sqrt{0.8}$

16. $-\sqrt{50}$

Evaluate $\sqrt{b^2 - 4ac}$ for the given values of a, b, and c.

17. $a = -5$, $b = 4$, $c = 1$

18. $a = 6$, $b = 4$, $c = 2$

19. $a = -7$, $b = 5$, $c = 2$

20. $a = 3$, $b = 10$, $c = 3$

21. $a = -6$, $b = 4$, $c = 2$

22. $a = 3$, $b = 4$, $c = -7$

Solving quadratic equations by finding square roots

A quadratic equation is an equation in the standard form of: $ax^2 + bx + c = 0$, $a \neq 0$.
In this form a is considered the leading coefficient. As part of this equation, if $b = 0$,
solve simply $x^2 = d$ by following these three guidelines.

1. If d is positive, then $x^2 = d$ will have two solutions. $x = \pm \sqrt{d}$
2. If d is 0, then $x^2 = 0$ will have only one solution. $x = 0$
3. If d is negative, then $x = d$ will have no solution.

Solve $x^2 = 121$	Solve $x^2 = -9$	Solve $4x^2 - 100 = 0$
$x = \pm 11$	x has no solution.	$4x^2 = 100$
		$x^2 = 25$
		$x = \pm 5$

Write each quadratic equation in standard form and state the leading coefficient.

1. $3x + x^2 - 5 = 0$

2. $10 = 7x^2 - 5x$

3. $4x^2 - 6x = 15$

4. $5x^2 - 6 = 4x$

5. $8x - x^2 + 12 = 0$

6. $8 - 9x^2 + 5x = 0$

Solve each equation.

7. $x^2 = 16$

8. $3x^2 = 507$

9. $x^2 - 40 = 60$

10. $8x^2 = 800$

11. $2x^2 = 128$

12. $4x^2 + 16 = 500$

13. $x^2 = 49$

14. $x^2 + 2 = 83$

15. $25x^2 + 9 = 45$

Use a calculator to solve each equation. Round to 2 decimal places.

16. $4x^2 + 2 = 68$

17. $x^2 - 12 = 0$

18. $\frac{1}{2}x^2 - 12 = 21$

19. $6x^2 - 10 = 20$

20. $5x^2 - 10 = 30$

21. $\frac{1}{4}x^2 - 15 = 5$

22. $7x^2 + 14 = 63$

23. $3x^2 + 21 = 66$

24. $8x^2 + 25 = 105$

Name _____ Date _____

The quadratic formula

One way to solve any quadratic equation for its solutions is to use the quadratic formula. This formula is as follows:

$$x = \frac{-b \pm \sqrt{(b^2 - 4ac)}}{2a}$$, where x will be the solutions of the quadratic equation $ax^2 + bx + c = 0$.

Solve $x^2 + 3x + 2 = 0$
Since $a = 1$, $b = 3$, $c = 2$, substitute into the quadratic formula.

$$x = \frac{-3 \pm \sqrt{(3^2 - 4(1)(2))}}{2(1)} = \frac{-3 \pm \sqrt{(9 - 8)}}{2} = \frac{-3 \pm \sqrt{1}}{2} = \frac{-3 \pm 1}{2}$$

Thus, the equation has two solutions: $x = \frac{-3 + 1}{2} = -1$ and $x = \frac{-3 - 1}{2} = -2$

Note: It is important to remember that an equation must be written in standard form, $ax^2 + bx + c = 0$, before the quadratic formula can be applied.

Write each equation in standard form. Give the values of a, b, and c.

1. $3x - 5 + x^2 = 0$

2. $10 - x^2 = 0$

3. $12x - 5x^2 = 10$

4. $7x^2 + 12 = 5x$

5. $-4x^2 + 8x = 15$

6. $-3 - 4x = 2x^2$

Find the value of $b^2 - 4ac$ for each equation.

7. $3x^2 - 4x + 1 = 0$

8. $6x^2 - 5x + 1 = 0$

9. $5x^2 + 2x - 2 = 0$

10. $4x^2 - 3x - 5 = 0$

11. $x^2 - 11x + 3 = 0$

12. $-x^2 + 12x + 5 = 0$

Use the quadratic formula to solve each equation.

13. $3x^2 + 25x + 8 = 0$

14. $x^2 - 12x + 20 = 0$

15. $10x^2 + 19x + 6 = 0$

16. $x^2 + 9x + 20 = 0$

17. $8x^2 + 18x + 9 = 0$

18. $2x^2 + 7x + 3 = 0$

Graphing quadratic equations

Every quadratic equation $y = ax^2 + bx + c$ has a U-shaped graph called a parabola. Letting $y = 0$ and using the standard quadratic equation, $ax^2 + bx + c = 0$, if the leading coefficient a is positive, the graph will open up, and if the leading coefficient a is negative, the graph will open down. On a parabola that opens up, the lowest point is called the vertex. On a parabola that opens down, the highest point is the vertex. There is a vertical line that passes through the vertex called the axis of symmetry. This line divides the parabola into two equal images of each other. To sketch the graph of a parabola:

1. Find the x-coordinate of the vertex, which is $\frac{-b}{(2a)}$, and solve for the y-value.
   (Note: The axis of symmetry is the line $x = \frac{-b}{(2a)}$.)
2. Pick values of x to the right and to the left of the vertex x-coordinate and make a table of x and y values.
3. Plot the points and connect them to create the U-shaped parabola graph.

Sketch the graph of $y = x^2 - 2x + 3$.

vertex: x-value: $\frac{2}{(2(1))} = 1$

Create table of values using this y-value and the x-values to the right and left of this value.

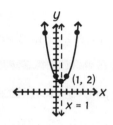

x	-2	0	1	2	4
$y = x^2 - 2x + 3$	11	3	2	3	11

Graph the parabola. The vertex is (1, 2), and the axis of symmetry is $x = 1$.
Connect the points with a U-shaped curve that opens up.

Find the coordinates of the vertex in each equation. State whether the graph **opens up** or **down**. Give the equation of the line of symmetry.

1. $y = 4x^2 + 4$

2. $y = x^2 + 8x + 3$

3. $y = x^2 + 4x + 16$

4. $y = x^2 - 6x + 1$

5. $y = -2x^2 - 12x - 4$

6. $y = 3x^2 - 18x + 2$

7. $y = -6x^2 + 2$

8. $y = -3x^2 + 6x - 1$

9. $y = -7x^2 - 2$

Sketch the graph of each equation. Label the vertex.

10. $y = x^2 - 2x + 2$

11. $y = x^2 - 6x + 4$

12. $y = x^2 + 8x + 10$

13. $y = -2x^2 - 4x + 1$

14. $y = -3x^2 - 5$

15. $y = 4x^2 - 16x + 12$

Name _____   Date _____

Introducing factoring

Factoring an integer means to express it as the product of two or more integers. If a number that is a positive integer has only positive factors of one and itself, it is called a prime number. If a number that is a positive integer has other positive factors, in addition to 1 and itself, it is called a composite number. Some prime numbers are 3, 5, 7, and 11. Some composite numbers are 4, 6, 12, and 20. Use these definitions to find what is called the prime factorization of a number.

Give the prime factorization of 30.

$30 = 2 \cdot 15 = 2 \cdot 3 \cdot 5$ (Stop when all numbers multiplied are prime.)

Thus, the prime factorization of 30 is: $2 \cdot 3 \cdot 5$.

The greatest common factor (GCF) of two or more integers is the largest integer that is a factor of all the integers.

Find the GCF of 48 and 72.

$48 = 3 \cdot 16 = 3 \cdot 4 \cdot 4 = 3 \cdot 2 \cdot 2 \cdot 2 \cdot 2 = 2^4 \cdot 3$

$72 = 2 \cdot 36 = 2 \cdot 6 \cdot 6 = 2 \cdot 2 \cdot 3 \cdot 2 \cdot 3 = 2^3 \cdot 3^2$

Since 2^3 and 3 are common to both of these integers, the GCF is 24.

Give the prime factorization of each number.

1. 8   **2.** 10   **3.** 150   **4.** 45

5. 9   **6.** 40   **7.** 90   **8.** 60

9. 14   **10.** 28   **11.** 360   **12.** 200

Find the GCF of each group of numbers.

13. 12, 18, 36   **14.** $16x^8, 24x^7$ **15.** $12x^6, 15x^3, 2x^2, 9x^4$

16. 35, 70, 105   **17.** $4x^5, 12x^7, 36x^4$ **18.** $7x^2y^2, 7x^3y^5, 14x^2y^4$

19. $5a^2, 10a^3, 15a^4$ **20.** $6x^3, 9x^5, 27x^4$ **21.** $3x^2, 6x^3y^3, 12x^4$

Greatest common monomial factor

The greatest common factor (GCF) of a polynomial is the greatest common factor of its terms.

Factor out the GCF from $6x^5 + 12x^4 + 24x^2$.

First, find the GCF of 6, 12, and 24, which is 6.

Second, find the GCF of x^5, x^4, and x^2, which would be the least of the three powers. So this GCF is x^2. Combined, the GCF of the polynomial is $6x^2$.

Third, write each term as a product of $6x^2$ and a monomial.

$$6x^5 + 12x^4 + 24x^2 = 6x^2(x^3) + 6x^2(2x^2) + 6x^2(4)$$
$$= 6x^2(x^3 + 2x^2 + 4) \text{ Final factorization of the polynomial}$$

State the GCF of each polynomial.

1. $4x^2 - 8$

2. $x^4 + x^3$

3. $4x^2 + 10x$

4. $4x^2 + 3x^4 + 2x^5$

5. $6x - 12$

6. $6x^4 - 3x^3$

7. $5x^4 + 15x^2$

8. $5x^4 - 10x^2 + 20x$

Factor out the GCF from each polynomial.

9. $4x(x^2) - 4x(6x) + 4x(8)$

10. $3x^2(3x^2) - 3x^2(4x) + 3x^2(5)$

11. $6x(3x^2) + 6x(8x) - 6x(4)$

12. $5x^2(2x^2) - 5x^2(7x) - 5x^2(6)$

13. $x^4(x^2) + x^4(x) + x^4(1)$

14. $6x(2x^2) - 6x(4x) + 6x(3)$

Factor out the GCF from each polynomial.

15. $4x^2 - 8x + 12$

16. $x^7 + x^6 - x^5$

17. $4x^3 - 16x^2 - 48x$

18. $25x^2 + 30x - 55$

19. $44x^3 - 11x^2$

20. $8x^6 + 4x^4 - 12x^2$

21. $3x^3 + 9x^2 - 12x$

22. $7x^2 - 21x$

23. $xy^2 - xy - 16x$

24. $6x^3 - 15x^2$

25. $9x^6 + 81x^3 - 27x$

26. $2x^2 y + 4x - 6y$

Factoring in two special cases

Factoring can be seen as the reverse process of multiplying. When factoring polynomials, it is important to remember two special cases.

1. Difference of two squares: $a^2 - b^2 = (a + b)(a - b)$

    $25 - 4x^2 = (5 + 2x)(5 - 2x)$ $6x^2 - 100y^2 = (6x + 10y)(6x - 10y)$

2. Perfect square trinomials: $a^2 + 2ab + b = (a + b)^2$

    $a^2 - 2ab + b = (a - b)^2$

    $x^2 + 10x + 25 = (x + 5)^2$ $x^2 - 12x + 36 = (x - 6)^2$

note: The perfect square trinomials can come in two forms: one with the coefficient of the middle term positive and one with the coefficient negative.

Factor each polynomial.

1. $x^2 - 100$

2. $64 - x^2$

3. $9 - x^2$

4. $1 - 81x^2$

5. $x^2 - 49$

6. $x^2 - 625$

7. $225x^2 - 16$

8. $9x^2 - 25$

Factor each perfect square. If not a perfect square, write **not a perfect square**.

9. $x^2 + 10x + 25$

10. $x^2 - 14x + 49$

11. $25x^2 - 8x + 1$

12. $4x^2 - 12x + 36$

13. $9x^2 + 6x + 1$

14. $x^2 - 4x + 4$

Factor each polynomial using a special case or write **not special**.

15. $121x^2 - 64y^2$

16. $9xy^2 + 54xy + 81y^2$

17. $25x^2 - 225y^2$

18. $16x^2 - (3y - 1)^2$

19. $49x^2 + 70xy + 25y^2$

20. $(2y + 7)^2 - 169x^2$

21. $4x^2 - 40xy + 100y^2$

22. $36x^2 - 49y^2$

Factoring quadratic trinomials in the form $x^2 + bx + c$

Quadratic Equations and Factoring

To factor a trinomial means to express it as the product of two binomials. To factor $x^2 + bx + c$, look for two numbers that are the product of c and whose sum is b.

Factor $x^2 + 3x - 4$.

     First, set up the factor process like this. $(x\quad)(x\quad)$

     Second, put your signs in the factors. $(x +\quad)(x -\quad)$
          (The signs are + and – because c is negative.)

     Third, find the two numbers that are a product of -4 and whose sum is 3.
          $4 \cdot -1 = -4$ and $4 + -1 = 3$ Thus, the two numbers are 4 and -1.

     Fourth, write in the final factors. $(x + 4)(x - 1)$

note: If c is positive and b is positive, then the factors will both be positive. If c is positive and b is negative, then the factors will both be negative. If c is negative, the factors will have opposite signs.

In each trinomial, state all possible factors of its constant term. Give the signs of each factor that will be used in each binomial.

1. $x^2 + 5x + 6$ **2.** $x^2 - 2x - 35$ **3.** $x^2 - 15x + 56$ **4.** $x^2 - 12x + 20$

5. $x^2 + 3x + 2$ **6.** $x^2 + 14x + 45$ **7.** $x^2 + 3x - 28$ **8.** $x^2 - x - 30$

9. $x^2 - 4x + 4$ **10.** $x^2 + 10x + 16$ **11.** $x^2 + 6x - 40$ **12.** $x^2 + 9x - 22$

Factor each trinomial.

13. $x^2 + 10x - 24$ **14.** $x^2 - 18x - 40$ **15.** $x^2 + 5x - 36$ **16.** $x^2 + 16x - 17$

17. $x^2 + 8x + 7$ **18.** $x^2 - x - 20$ **19.** $x^2 - 2x + 1$ **20.** $x^2 - 10x + 21$

21. $x^2 - 7x + 10$ **22.** $x^2 + 19x + 34$ **23.** $x^2 - 2x - 48$ **24.** $x^2 + 3x - 54$

25. $x^2 - 6x - 16$ **26.** $x^2 - 4x - 21$ **27.** $x^2 + 15x + 56$ **28.** $x^2 - 11x + 30$

Factoring quadratic trinomials in the form $ax^2 + bx + c$

Factoring quadratic trinomials of the form $ax^2 + bx + c$ involves a trial and error process. Some clues can be determined from the signs of b and c in finding the binomial factors, but basically work these problems on a trial basis.

Factor $3x^2 + x - 10$.

First, because c is negative and b is positive, look for factors of 10 that will be positive and negative.

The factors of $3x^2$ have to be $3x$ and x. So, set up the factoring:
$$(3x \quad)(x \quad)$$

Now, the factors of 10: try 5 and -2.

$(3x + 5)(x - 2)$ Does this work? Check $3x(x) + 5x - 6x - 10$
No, this gives us $3x^2 - x - 10$.

$(3x - 5)(x + 2)$ Try again just switching the signs.
Check $3x(x) - 5x + 6x - 10 = 3x^2 + x - 10$

Thus, the factors of $3x^2 + x - 10$ are $(3x - 5)(x + 2)$.

Note: You could find yourself trying several different combinations before finding the correct pair of binomial factors.

State all possible factors of a and c in each trinomial.

1. $3x^2 + 8x - 10$ **2.** $6x^2 + 5x + 11$ **3.** $10x^2 - 12x - 5$ **4.** $28x^2 + 7x - 9$

5. $8x^2 - 6x + 12$ **6.** $12x^2 - 6x + 7$ **7.** $7x^2 + 5x - 35$ **8.** $16x^2 - x + 4$

Factor each trinomial using the trial and error method.

9. $3x^2 - 7x - 6$ **10.** $12x^2 + 24x - 15$ **11.** $9x^2 - 6x - 3$

12. $8x^2 + 22x + 15$ **13.** $8x^2 - 22x - 6$ **14.** $10x^2 - 22x - 24$

15. $5x^2 + 9x - 2$ **16.** $14x^2 + 39x - 35$ **17.** $6x^2 - 10x - 56$

18. Give an example of a trinomial with a leading coefficient other than 1, and show how it can be factored.

Factoring combining different types of methods

To factor a polynomial completely means to factor it into irreducible polynomials that have no common factor. Several steps can help in this process.

1. Look to see if there is a GCF.
2. Look for a special case, such as difference of two squares and perfect square trinomial.
3. If not a special case, look for two different binomial factors.

Factor $3x^4 + 12x^3 + 9x^2$

1. Is there a GCF?   Yes, $3x^2$.
        $3x^2(x^2 + 4x + 3)$ Factor $3x^2$ out.
2. Is there a special case?   no.
3. Can $x^2 + 4x + 3$ be factored into two binomials? Yes.
        $x^2 + 4x + 3 = (x + 3)(x + 1)$

Thus, $3x^4 + 12x^3 + 9x^2 = 3x^2(x + 3)(x + 1)$

State the method you would use to factor each polynomial: **(1)** as a product of two binomials, **(2)** as a perfect square trinomial, **(3)** as the difference of two squares, or **(4)** by factoring out a monomial.

1. $x^2 - 36$

2. $x^2 + 8x + 16$

3. $4x + 4y + 3x + 3y$

4. $9x^2 - 25y^2$

5. $x^2 + 4x - 21$

6. $x^2 + 7x + 12$

7. $x^4 + 2x^3 - x^2 + 20x$

8. $x^2 - 10x + 25$

Factor each polynomial completely.

9. $2x^2 + 20x + 32$

10. $6x^2 - 18xy - 60y^2$

11. $50x^2 - 72y^2$

12. $7x^4 + 8x^3 + 5x^5 + 6x^6$

13. $3x^3y - 9x^2y + 6xy^3 - 15xy^2$

14. $20x^3 - 6x^2 - 8x$

15. $16x^2 - 16y^2$

16. $16x^2 - 16x + 4$

17. $x^3 - 7x^2y + 6xy^2$

Algebra

Solving quadratic equations by factoring

To connect factoring and solving equations, it is important to understand the zero-product property. This property states: if the product $ab = 0$, then $a = 0$ or $b = 0$.

1. Solve the equation $(x + 3)(x - 2) = 0$.

   Use the zero-product property and set both factors equal to 0 and solve.

   $$x + 3 = 0 \quad \text{or} \quad x - 2 = 0$$
   $$x = -3 \qquad\qquad x = 2$$

Thus, the equation $(x + 3)(x - 2) = 0$ has two solutions: -3 and 2.

2. Solve $x^2 + 7x + 12 = 0$.

   $$\begin{aligned} &(x + 4)(x + 3) = 0 && \text{First, factor.} \\ &x + 4 = 0 \quad \text{or} \quad x + 3 = 0 && \text{Zero-product property} \\ &x = -4 \quad \text{or} \quad x = -3 && \text{Solve for } x. \end{aligned}$$

Thus, $x^2 + 7x + 12 = 0$ has two solutions: -4 and -3.

Note: Always check the solutions in the original equation to make sure the correct solutions of the equation are found.

Find the solution set of each equation.

1. $(x - 3)(x + 2) = 0$

2. $x(x + 9) = 0$

3. $x(\frac{1}{4}x - 1)(\frac{1}{2}x + 2) = 0$

4. $(x - 8)(x + 7) = 0$

5. $(x - 10)(x - 1) = 0$

6. $x(\frac{1}{3}x + 5) = 0$

7. $(2x + 8)(x + 6) = 0$

8. $(x + 2)(x + 5) = 0$

9. $x(2x + 4)(x - 4) = 0$

10. $x(x - 1)(3x + 6)(x + 7) = 0$

Factor each trinomial. Find its solution set.

11. $x^2 - 64 = 0$

12. $4x^3 - 16x = 0$

13. $4x^2 - 25 = 0$

14. $3x^3 + 4x^2 + x = 0$

15. $x^2 - 14x = 0$

16. $4x^2 + 32x + 64 = 0$

17. $2x^2 + x - 1 = 0$

18. $x^2 + 2x - 3 = 0$

19. $x^2 - 10x + 25 = 0$

Problem solving using quadratic equations

Quadratic Equations and Factoring

Problem solving often involves quadratic equations.

The square of a number is 8 less than 6 times the number. Find the numbers that make the sentence true.

$x^2 = 6x - 8$ First, set up the equation.
$x^2 - 6x + 8 = 0$ Put the equation in standard form.
$(x - 2)(x - 4) = 0$ Factor.
$x - 2 = 0$ or $x - 4 = 0$ Solve for x.
$x = 2$ or $x = 4$ Thus, the numbers are 2 and 4.

The product of a number and 10 more than 4 times the number is 50. Find the numbers that make the sentence true.

$x(4x + 10) = 50$ First, set up the equation.
$4x^2 + 10x - 50 = 0$ Put the equation in standard form.
$2(2x - 5)(x + 5) = 0$ Factor.
Since $2 \neq 0$, then $2x - 5 = 0$ or $x + 5 = 0$ Solve for x.
$x = \frac{5}{2}$ and $x = -5$ Thus, the numbers are $\frac{5}{2}$ and -5.

Write an equation for each problem. Solve to find the numbers that make each sentence true.

1. Six less than 3 times a number is 12 less than twice the number.

2. The square of a number is 8 more than twice the number.

3. The sum of the square of a number and 4 times the number is 12.

4. Twice the square of a number is 4 more than twice the number.

5. The product of a number and 6 more than twice the number is 20.

6. Three times the square of a number is 5 less than 16 times the number.

Review of Unit 10

Quadratic Equations and Factoring

Topics covered:

Square Roots

Solving Quadratic Equations by Finding Square Roots

The Quadratic Formula

Graphing Quadratic Equations

Introducing Factoring

Greatest Common Monomial Factor

Factoring in Two Special Cases

Factoring Quadratic Trinomials in the Form $x^2 + bx + c$

Factoring Quadratic Trinomials in the Form $ax^2 + bx + c$

Factoring Combining Different Types of Methods

Solving Quadratic Equations by Factoring

Problem Solving Using Quadratic Equations

Solve each equation. Round to the nearest hundredth when necessary.

1. $6x^2 = 150$

2. $x^2 - 5 = 76$

3. $36x^2 - 10 = 39$

4. $x^2 + 12 = 112$

Give the values of a, b, and c. Use the quadratic formula to solve each equation.

5. $x^2 - 6x + 8 = 0$

6. $x^2 + 8x + 12 = 0$

7. $x^2 - 2x - 8 = 0$

8. $2x^2 + 4x + 2 = 0$

9. $3x^2 + 6x - 9 = 0$

10. $2x^2 - 4x - 16 = 0$

11.–16. In problems 5–10, let the 0 in the equation be replaced by y. Then graph this quadratic equation. Label the vertex. For example, use $x^2 - 6x + 8 = 0$ to draw the parabola and label the vertex.

Find the GCF in each problem.

17. $5x^6 - 10x^4 - 15x^2$

18. 18, 45, 81

19. $x^{10} - x^7 + 2x^4$

20. $3x^4 - 9x^3 + 18x$

Factor each trinomial.

21. $x^2 - 5x + 6$

22. $x^2 - 3x - 28$

23. $9x^2 + 30xy + 25y^2$

24. $3x^2 + x - 10$

25. Factor $3x^3 - 9x^2 - 12x$ completely.

Solve.

26. $x^2 - 196 = 0$

27. If a number is multiplied by 4 more than twice a number, the result is 30. Find the numbers that ma[ke] the sentence true.

Unit 10 Test

Give the prime factorization of each number in each set. Find the GCF of each set of numbers.

1. 12, 48, 96

2. 18, 81, 117

3. 30, 60, 120, 150

4. 28, 49, 84

Solve each equation. Use the quadratic formula to solve problems 8–10.

5. $7x^2 = 70$

6. $36x^2 - 15 = 210$

7. $3x^2 - 4x - 4$

8. $x^2 - 12 = 37$

9. $x^2 - 7x + 12$

10. $x^2 + 12x + 27$

11. Graph $y = x^2 - 6x + 4$. Label the vertex. Does the graph open up or down?

Factor out the GCF in each polynomial.

12. $3x^7 - 9x^6 + 6x^4 - 15x^2$

13. $12x^2 - 24xy + 36xy^2$

14. $18x^3y^4 - 27x^4y^3 - 45x^4y^2$

Factor each trinomial completely.

15. $x^2 + 2x - 63$

16. $2x^3 + 6x^2 + 4x$

17. $9x^2 + 36xy + 36y^2$

18. $x^2 - 6x + 9$

19. $4x^2 + 10x - 6$

20. $x^2 - 5x - 36$

21. $49x^2 - 121y^2$

22. $3x^2 + 7x - 20$

23. $2x^3y - 72xy^3$

24. The square of a number is 5 more than 4 times the number. Find the numbers that make the sentence true.

25. A result of 35 is found when 2 times a number is added to the square of a number. Find the numbers that make the sentence true.

Simplifying rational expressions

A fraction whose numerator and denominator are polynomials is called a rational expression. To simplify rational expressions, follow two steps.

1. Factor the numerator and the denominator.
2. Divide any factors common to both the numerator and the denominator.

It is important to remember that an expression is undefined for a value if the value of a variable causes the denominator in the expression to be 0.

Find the values for which $\dfrac{x-4}{x^2+3x+2}$ is undefined.

$x^2 + 3x + 2$ First, set the denominator equal to 0.

$(x + 2)(x + 1)$ Factor denominator.

$x + 2 = 0$ or $x + 1 = 0$ Set each factor equal to 0.

$x = -2, \; x = -1$ Solve.

Thus, $\dfrac{x-4}{x^2+3x+2}$ is undefined for $x = -2$ or $x = -1$.

Simplify $\dfrac{3x - 12}{x^2 - x + 12}$

$\dfrac{3(x - 4)}{(x + 3)(x - 4)}$ Factor both the numerator and denominator.
Cancel out what is common to both.

$\dfrac{3}{x + 3}$ Simplified expression

Find the value(s) of x that would make the rational expression undefined.

1. $\dfrac{x - 4}{3x + 9}$

2. $\dfrac{x}{2x + 6}$

3. $\dfrac{x}{x^2 + 8x + 7}$

4. $\dfrac{5x + 6}{x^2 + 3x - 18}$

5. $\dfrac{-14}{6x - 12}$

6. $\dfrac{x - 15}{4x - 16}$

7. $\dfrac{x - 4}{x^2 - 5x - 6}$

8. $\dfrac{x - 9}{x^2 - 10x + 25}$

Simplify each expression.

9. $\dfrac{16x}{24}$

10. $\dfrac{15x}{60x^4}$

11. $\dfrac{x - 7}{x^2 - 7x}$

12. $\dfrac{x^2 + 7x}{x^2 + 5x - 14}$

13. $\dfrac{-36x}{84x}$

14. $\dfrac{2x - 12}{x - 6}$

15. $\dfrac{x^2 - 36}{x^2 + 4x - 12}$

16. $\dfrac{6x - 24}{x^2 - 4x}$

Simplifying rational expressions to convenient form

Calculating Rational Expressions

A rational expression is said to be simplified in convenient form if:
1. The expression is written in descending order of exponents.
2. The first coefficient, or leading coefficient, is positive.

Write $-3x^2 + x + 9 - x^3$ in convenient form.

$-x^3 - 3x^2 + x + 9$	Write in descending order of exponents.
$-1(x^3 + 3x^2 - x - 9)$	Factor out -1 to obtain a positive first coefficient.
$-1(x^3 + 3x^2 - x - 9)$	Convenient form

Simplify

$\dfrac{-2 + 5x - 3x^2}{-4 + 8x - 3x^2}$	
$\dfrac{-3x^2 + 5x - 2}{-3x^2 + 8x - 4}$	Rewrite the numerator and denominator in descending order of exponents.
$\dfrac{-1(3x^2 - 5x + 2)}{-1(3x^2 - 8x + 4)}$	Factor out -1 to obtain a positive first coefficient.
$\dfrac{-1(3x - 2)(x - 1)}{-1(3x - 2)(x - 2)}$	Factor the numerator and denominator. Cancel out what is common to both.
$\dfrac{x - 1}{x - 2}$	Simplified convenient form

Change each expression to convenient form.

1. $-6x - 5$

2. $36 - x^2$

3. $52 + y - x^2$

4. $11 - 2x + 2x^2$

5. $-x^2 + 10$

6. $-x^2 + 5x - 7$

7. $-x^2 + 9x - 4$

8. $-9x - 7$

Simplify each expression. Write each answer in convenient form.

9. $\dfrac{10 - x}{5x - 50}$

10. $\dfrac{x - 1}{1 - x^2}$

11. $\dfrac{18x^2 - 3x}{-6x^2 + 7x - 1}$

12. $\dfrac{2 - x}{x^2 + 4x - 12}$

13. $\dfrac{x^2 - 5x + 6}{3 - x}$

14. $\dfrac{9 - x}{x^2 - 8x - 9}$

15. $\dfrac{4x^3 - 16x^2 + 12x}{12x - 4x^2}$

16. $\dfrac{-2x^2 - x + 6}{x^2 - 2x - 8}$

Evaluate each expression for its given x-value.

17. $-x^2 + 2x - 16$ for $x = 2$

18. $\dfrac{-6 - x}{x^2 + 3x - 1}$ for $x = -1$

Multiplying rational expressions

When multiplying rational expressions, follow these three steps.

1. Multiply the numerators.
2. Multiply the denominators.
3. Write the new fraction in reduced form.

Multiply $\dfrac{7x^3}{4y^2} \cdot \dfrac{2y^3}{8x^5}$

$7x^3 \cdot 2y^3 = 14x^3y^3$ Multiply the numerators.

$14y^2 \cdot 8x^5 = 32x^5y^2$ Multiply the denominators.

$\dfrac{14x^3y^3}{32x^5y^2}$ Write the new fraction.

$\dfrac{7y}{16x^2}$ Write the new fraction in reduced form.

note: It is faster to cancel factors in the numerator and the denominator before multiplying.

Multiply $\dfrac{x^2 - 2x - 8}{x^2 - 2x - 3} \cdot \dfrac{x - 3}{x + 2}$

$\dfrac{(x + 2)(x - 4)}{(x - 3)(x + 1)} \cdot \dfrac{x - 3}{x + 2}$ Factor the numerators and denominators.

$\dfrac{\cancel{(x + 2)}(x - 4)}{\cancel{(x - 3)}(x + 1)} \cdot \dfrac{\cancel{x - 3}}{\cancel{x + 2}}$ Cancel out the common factors.

$\dfrac{x - 4}{x + 1} \cdot 1$ Rewrite the remaining factors. Multiply.

$\dfrac{x - 4}{x + 1}$ Final product

Multiply.

1. $\dfrac{8}{11} \cdot \dfrac{5}{9}$

2. $\dfrac{x - 8}{x + 2} \cdot x - 8$

3. $\dfrac{4x^4y^6}{x^2 - 9} \cdot \dfrac{6 - 2x}{8x^6y^4}$

4. $\dfrac{3}{10} \cdot \dfrac{-9}{13}$

5. $\dfrac{x + 2}{22} \cdot \dfrac{11}{x + 2}$

6. $(x + 4) \cdot \dfrac{3x - 6}{x^2 + 2x - 8}$

7. $\dfrac{7a}{5} \cdot \dfrac{a^3}{4}$

8. $\dfrac{-6x}{6x - 12} \cdot \dfrac{3x - 6}{12x^3}$

9. $\dfrac{16x^7y}{7 - x} \cdot \dfrac{3x - 21}{32x^4y^6}$

10. $\dfrac{6x}{17y^2} \cdot \dfrac{4y^8}{3x^9}$

11. $\dfrac{45}{6x + 8y} \cdot \dfrac{9x + 12y}{9}$

12. $\dfrac{x^2 - y^2}{3x^2 - 21xy + 30y^2} \cdot \dfrac{75y^2 - 3x^2}{x^2 - 2xy + y^2}$

13. $\dfrac{-5x^5}{9y^2} \cdot \dfrac{12y^{10}}{10x^7}$

14. $\dfrac{4x - 24}{4x^2 + 18x - 10} \cdot (2x - 1)$

Dividing rational expressions

To divide one rational expression by another, multiply the first by the reciprocal of the second. Be sure not to confuse the operation. Invert the divisor (the second fraction) only.

Divide

$$\frac{15x^6}{5y^5} \div \frac{3x^4}{5y^4}$$

$$\frac{\cancel{15}x^6 \cdot \,^2}{\cancel{5}y^8} \cdot \frac{5y^4}{3x^4}$$ Change to multiplication.
Cancel common factors.

$$\frac{5x^2}{y} \cdot 1$$ Multiply.

$$\frac{5x^2}{y}$$ Final product

Divide

$$\frac{x^2 + 9x + 20}{x^2 - 5x + 6} \div \frac{x + 4}{x - 2}$$

$$\frac{x^2 + 9x + 20}{x^2 - 5x + 6} \cdot \frac{x - 2}{x + 4}$$ Change to multiplication.

$$\frac{(x + 4)(x + 5)}{(x - 3)(x - 2)} \cdot \frac{x - 2}{x + 4}$$ Factor the numerator and denominator and cancel common factors.

$$\frac{x + 5}{x - 3} \cdot 1$$ Multiply.

$$\frac{x + 5}{x - 3}$$ Final product

Give the reciprocal of each rational expression.

1. 10

2. $x + 12$

3. $\frac{3}{4}$

4. $x^2 - 7$

5. $\frac{1}{x - 4}$

6. $\frac{3x^2}{x^2 - 5x + 8}$

7. 0

8. $\frac{4x^2 - 3x + 7}{5x - 12}$

Divide.

9. $\frac{8}{9} \div \frac{1}{9}$

10. $\frac{15x^7y^6}{4x - 8x^2} \div \frac{24x^6y^8}{8x - 4}$

11. $\frac{4x^2 - 25y^2}{2x^2y + 5xy^2} \div \frac{6x^2 - 15xy}{9x^2y^2}$

12. $\frac{x^2}{y^3} \div \frac{y^3}{x^5}$

13. $\frac{x^2 - 2x - 15}{5x^2 + 15x} \div x^2 - 6x + 5$

14. $\frac{x^2 - x - 12}{x^2 + x - 6} \div \frac{x^2 - 2x - 8}{x^2 - x - 2}$

15. $\frac{3xy^2}{-5z^5} \div \frac{6xz^2}{10y^3}$

16. $\frac{x - 8}{4} \div \frac{x + 8}{8}$

17. $\frac{x^2 - 81}{x^2 - 3x - 54} \div \frac{2x + 18}{6x + 36}$

18. $\frac{4x - 12}{12} \div \frac{x^2 - 9}{24}$

19. $\frac{x^2 - 25}{x - 3} \div \frac{5x + 25}{2x - 6}$

20. $\frac{2x^2 + 5x + 3}{x^2 + 9x + 14} \div \frac{2x^2 - 3x - 9}{x^2 + 6x - 7}$

Name _____   Date _____

Adding and subtracting with like denominators

When adding and subtracting rational expressions with like denominators, add/subtract the numerators and write the result as a fraction with the common denominator.

Add $\dfrac{8x}{4} + \dfrac{5x}{4}$

$8x + 5x$ — Add the numerators.

$\dfrac{13x}{4}$ — Write as a fraction with the common denominator.

Subtract $\dfrac{5x}{x-2} - \dfrac{4x}{x-2}$

$5x - 4x$ — Subtract the numerators.

$\dfrac{x}{x-2}$ — Write as a fraction with the common denominator.

note: Before adding and subtracting rational expressions, the expressions need to be in convenient form.

Add $\dfrac{x^2}{x^2 + 2x - 8} + \dfrac{-3x + 10}{-x^2 - 2x + 8}$

$\dfrac{x^2}{x^2 + 2x - 8} - \dfrac{-3x + 10}{+(x^2 + 2x - 8)}$ — Write $-x^2 - 2x + 8$ in convenient form. $-1(x^2 + 2x - 8)$ -1 means addition changes to subtraction. Factor denominators only.

$\dfrac{x^2 + 3x + 10}{(x + 4)(x - 2)} = \dfrac{(x + 5)(x - 2)}{(x + 4)(x - 2)}$ — Subtract numerators. Then factor if possible. Cancel common factors.

$\dfrac{x + 5}{x + 4}$ — Final answer

note: When subtracting an expression, remember to distribute the negative sign to each term in the expression.

Add or subtract each expression.

1. $\dfrac{9x}{4} + \dfrac{8x}{4}$

2. $\dfrac{2x}{5} - \dfrac{x-1}{5}$

3. $\dfrac{x}{2x-6} - \dfrac{3}{2x-6}$

4. $\dfrac{5x^2}{6} + \dfrac{8x^2}{6}$

5. $\dfrac{4x}{2x} - \dfrac{2x+2}{2x}$

6. $\dfrac{6x}{x^2 + 8x} + \dfrac{48}{x^2 + 8x}$

7. $\dfrac{x}{x-5} + \dfrac{5}{5-x}$

8. $\dfrac{3}{x} + \dfrac{2}{x} - \dfrac{1}{x}$

9. $\dfrac{3x}{x^2 + 2x - 15} + \dfrac{15}{x^2 + 2x - 15}$

10. $\dfrac{x+12}{x} - \dfrac{5}{x}$

11. $\dfrac{8x}{x-6} + \dfrac{3x}{6-x}$

12. $\dfrac{2x^2}{x-1} + \dfrac{2}{1-x}$

Find the perimeter of each figure.

13.

$\dfrac{6x}{5}$ $\quad$ $\dfrac{x}{5}$

14.

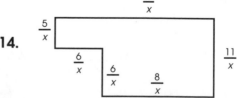

$\dfrac{12}{x}$, $\dfrac{5}{x}$, $\dfrac{6}{x}$, $\dfrac{6}{x}$, $\dfrac{8}{x}$, $\dfrac{11}{x}$

Adding and subtracting with unlike denominators

To add and subtract expressions with unlike denominators, first find the LCD (least common denominator). The LCD is found by factoring each denominator into prime factors and identifying the most number of times each factor must occur.

$\frac{3}{4x} + \frac{7}{16x}$ Find the LCD of $4x$ and $16x$. (The LCD is the least common multiple of $4x$ and 16.)

$4x = 2 \cdot 2 \cdot x$
$16x = 2 \cdot 2 \cdot 2 \cdot 2 \cdot x$

Since 2 most occurs 4 times and x most occurs once, the LCD is $2 \cdot 2 \cdot 2 \cdot 2 \cdot x = 16x$. Once the LCD is found, multiply each term by the factors in the LCD it is missing. Be sure to multiply the numerator and the denominator of each term by the same factors.

Add $\frac{1}{3x^3} + \frac{7}{2x^2} + \frac{3}{6x}$

$3x^3 = 3 \cdot x \cdot x \cdot x$ Find the prime factors of each denominator.
$2x^2 = 2 \cdot x \cdot x$
$6x = 2 \cdot 3 \cdot x$

$2 \cdot 3 \cdot x \cdot x \cdot x = 6x^3$ Common denominator

$\frac{2}{2}\left(\frac{1}{3x^3}\right) + \frac{3x}{3x}\left(\frac{7}{2x^2}\right) + \frac{x^2}{x^2}\left(\frac{3}{6x}\right)$ Multiply the numerator and denominator of each term by the LCD factors the denominator is missing. Rewrite with the common denominator.

$\frac{2 + 21x + 3x^2}{6x^3}$

$\frac{3x^2 + 21x + 2}{6x^3}$ Simplify.

Find the LCD of each set of fractions.

1. $\frac{5}{2} + \frac{3}{5} - \frac{3}{4}$

2. $\frac{4x}{3x^3} + \frac{x}{x^2} - \frac{6}{8x}$

3. $\frac{9x}{4xy} - \frac{12x}{6x}$

4. $\frac{4x-5}{3x^2} - \frac{5x-1}{4x^3}$

5. $\frac{4x+3}{3} - \frac{3x+2}{7}$

6. $\frac{1}{3x^4} - \frac{4}{x^6} + \frac{3}{6x^2}$

Add or subtract each expression. Each answer should be in the simplest form.

7. $\frac{6x}{15} + \frac{2x}{5}$

8. $\frac{7}{24x} + \frac{3x-4}{6x} + \frac{x+3}{4x}$

9. $\frac{7}{5x^2} - \frac{1}{10x} + \frac{9}{4x^4}$

10. $\frac{3x}{4} - \frac{x}{2}$

11. $\frac{1}{x^3} + \frac{2}{x} - \frac{3}{4x^2}$

12. $\frac{3x+8}{6x} + \frac{3x-2}{4x}$

13. Find the perimeter of the figure.

Adding and subtracting with polynomial denominators

Adding and subtracting rational expressions will often involve polynomial denominators. The first step to take when solving such problems is to find the LCD. Then replace the rational expressions with equivalent expressions that have the LCD as the denominator.

1. Add $\dfrac{5}{x-2} + \dfrac{7}{x-6}$

$(x-2)(x-6)$

$\dfrac{(x-6)}{(x-6)} \cdot \dfrac{5}{x-2} + \dfrac{(x-2)}{(x-2)} \cdot \dfrac{7}{x-6}$

$\dfrac{5x-30+7x-14}{(x-2)(x-6)}$

$\dfrac{12x-44}{(x-2)(x-6)} = \dfrac{4(3x-11)}{(x-2)(x-6)}$

Since $x-2$ and $x-6$ are both irreducible, the LCD is $(x-2)(x-6)$.
Multiply the numerator and the denominator of each term by its missing factor.
Rewrite with the LCD.

Add and find the final result.

2. Subtract $(x+2) - \dfrac{(x-1)}{2x+1}$

1 and $2x+1$; LCD $= 2x+1$

$\dfrac{2x+1}{2x+1}(x+2) - \dfrac{(x-1)}{2x+1}$

$\dfrac{2x^2+5x+2-x+1}{2x+1}$

$\dfrac{2x^2+4x+3}{2x+1}$

Find the LCD.

Multiply the numerator and the denominator of each term by its missing factor.

Rewrite with the LCD.

Add like terms and find the final result.

Find the LCD of each set of fractions.

1. $\dfrac{4}{x-3} + \dfrac{-3}{x+2}$

2. $\dfrac{4}{x-1} + \dfrac{3}{x+6}$

3. $12 + \dfrac{3}{x}$

4. $(x+4) + \dfrac{8}{x-3}$

5. $\dfrac{6}{2x+3} - \dfrac{7}{x-4}$

6. $3 - \dfrac{5}{x}$

7. $\dfrac{5}{x^2} + 1$

8. $(x-1) - \dfrac{3x}{x+2}$

Add or subtract each expression.

9. $\dfrac{4}{x-3} + \dfrac{2}{x}$

10. $\dfrac{3x}{x^2-36} - \dfrac{18}{6-x}$

11. $(x+4) + \dfrac{x-5}{4x-3}$

12. $6 - \dfrac{1}{x+6}$

13. $\dfrac{x}{x-4} - \dfrac{10}{x+4}$

14. $\dfrac{5}{x-7} - \dfrac{4}{x^2-5x-14}$

Name _____   Date _____

Review of Unit 11

Topics covered:

Simplifying Rational Expressions
Simplifying Rational Expressions
   to Convenient Form
Multiplying Rational Expressions
Dividing Rational Expressions

Adding and Subtracting with Like Denominators
Adding and Subtracting with Unlike Denominators
Adding and Subtracting with Polynomial Denominators

1. Describe what is meant when a rational expression is undefined.

2. How do you find when a rational expression is undefined?

3. Give a definition of the LCD of a set of fractions. When do you need an LCD?

4. Explain how to add or subtract a polynomial and a rational expression. Use $(x - 2) + \dfrac{4x}{x+4}$ to help you explain.

5. For what values of x is the expression $\dfrac{4x - 1}{x^2 - 3x - 10}$ undefined?

Simplify each expression.

6. $\dfrac{48x^6}{16x^8}$

7. $\dfrac{x^2 + 7x + 12}{x^2 - 2x - 15}$

8. $\dfrac{x^2 - 64}{x + 8}$

9. $\dfrac{x - 6}{6 + 5x - x^2}$

Multiply or divide.

10. $\dfrac{15x^4y^6}{6 - x} \cdot \dfrac{x^2 - 36}{5xy^8}$

11. $\dfrac{x^2 + 5x - 14}{x + 2} \cdot \dfrac{6x + 12}{x^2 + 4x - 21}$

12. $\dfrac{45x^9y^5}{48 - 3x^2} \div \dfrac{15x^7y^9}{4x + 16}$

Add or subtract.

13. $\dfrac{2x}{x + 5} + \dfrac{10}{x + 5}$

14. $\dfrac{3x}{x^2 - 6x + 9} - \dfrac{9}{x^2 - 6x + 9}$

15. $\dfrac{3}{8x^2} + \dfrac{7}{24x^3}$

16. Find the perimeter.

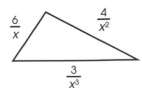

17. Find the area.

$x^2 + 8x + 12$

$\dfrac{1}{x + 6}$

Unit 11 Test

1. What is the definition of a rational expression? Give an example.

2. When is a rational expression undefined? Give an example.

3. What is meant when saying a rational expression is in convenient form? Give an example.

4. When is an LCD needed when performing operations involving rational expressions?

Name the values of the variable x that make each rational expression in 5–8 undefined?

5. $\dfrac{x-4}{2x+8}$

6. $\dfrac{x+7}{8-x}$

7. $\dfrac{x+5}{x^2+3x-54}$

8. $\dfrac{x-10}{x^2-9x}$

Multiply or divide.

9. $\dfrac{12x^3y^6}{5z^7} \cdot \dfrac{15x^3y^2}{3z^2}$

10. $\dfrac{x^2-2x-48}{x^2-64} \div \dfrac{x^2+2x-24}{4x+32}$

11. $\dfrac{x^2+9x+20}{x+3} \cdot \dfrac{5x+15}{x+5}$

12. $\dfrac{x^2+3x+2}{x^2-4x-5} \div \dfrac{x^2+4x-12}{x^2+x-30}$

Add or subtract.

13. $\dfrac{4x}{x+7} + \dfrac{28}{x+7}$

14. $\dfrac{x+4}{x+6} + \dfrac{3x-8}{x^2-x-42}$

15. $\dfrac{-2}{x-3} - 5$

16. $\dfrac{4x-3}{2} - \dfrac{5x+7}{3} + \dfrac{4x}{6}$

17. Find the perimeter.

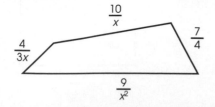

18. Find the area.

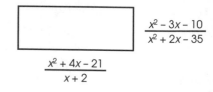

Ratios and proportions

A ratio is a comparison of two numbers by division. For example, $\frac{3}{x}$ is a ratio.
When two ratios are set equal to each other, this is called a proportion. For example,
$\frac{3}{x} = \frac{2}{3}$ is a proportion. There are two properties of proportions to remember.

1. If two ratios are equal, then their reciprocals are equal.
    if $\frac{6}{2} = \frac{12}{4}$, then $\frac{2}{6} = \frac{4}{12}$.
2. The product of the extremes equals the product of the means.
    Example, if $\frac{3}{x} = \frac{1}{4}$, then $3(4) = x(1)$.
    The extremes are 3 and 4, and the means are x and 1.

Problems that involve proportions often involve a variable. When solving for the variable, the proportion is actually being solved.

Solve $\frac{x}{(x+6)} = \frac{3}{x}$

extremes: x and x; means: $x + 6$ and 3	First, identify the extremes and the means.
$3(x + 6) = x(x)$	Cross multiply.
$3x + 18 = x^2$	Simplify.
$x^2 - 3x - 18 = 0$	Write in standard form.
$(x - 6)(x + 3) = 0$	Factor.
$x = 6$ and $x = -3$	Solve for x.

Thus, the solution of this proportion is 6 and -3.

Identify the extremes and the means in each proportion.

1. $\frac{4}{15} = \frac{3x}{10}$

2. $\frac{x}{4} = \frac{8}{3}$

3. $\frac{x}{2} = \frac{3}{x+2}$

4. $\frac{x+4}{6} = \frac{x+7}{7}$

5. $\frac{5}{6} = \frac{45}{n}$

6. $\frac{11}{x} = \frac{44}{121}$

7. $\frac{x}{3} = \frac{4}{x-5}$

8. $\frac{4}{x+8} = \frac{3}{x}$

Solve each proportion.

9. $\frac{x}{4} = \frac{21}{7}$

10. $\frac{9}{3} = \frac{6}{x}$

11. $\frac{x-3}{4} = \frac{x-4}{3}$

12. $\frac{x}{4} = \frac{8}{2x}$

13. $\frac{12}{x} = 3$

14. $\frac{x}{5} = \frac{4}{x-1}$

15. $\frac{x}{2} = \frac{18}{x+5}$

16. $\frac{13}{x} = \frac{x}{13}$

17. What is the difference between a ratio and a proportion? Give a definition of both.

Rational equations

A rational equation contains one or more rational expressions separated with an equal sign. To solve a rational equation, follow these three steps.

1. Multiply each side of the equation by the least common denominator of each fraction in the equation.
2. Simplify each term in the equation.
3. Solve for x in the resulting polynomial equation using standard techniques.

Solve $\frac{5}{2x} + \frac{5}{x} = \frac{1}{3}$

$6x\left(\frac{5}{2x} + \frac{5}{x}\right) = \frac{1}{3}(6x)$ Multiply each side of the equation by LCD, $6x$.

$\frac{30x}{2x} + \frac{30x}{x} = \frac{6x}{3}$ Multiply each term by $6x$.

$15 + 30 = 2x$ Simplify.

$45 = 2x$ Divide by 2.

$x = 22\frac{1}{2}$ Solve for x.

note: When each side of an equation is a single fraction, use cross multiplying to solve the rational equation.

Solve $\frac{6}{x+4} = \frac{x}{2}$

$x(x+4) = 12$ Cross multiply.

$x^2 + 4x = 12$ Simplify.

$x^2 + 4x - 12 = 0$ Write the equation in standard form.

$(x+6)(x-2) = 0$ Factor.

$x = -6, x = 2$ Solve for x.

Thus, the solutions are -6 and 2.

Find the greatest common factor.

1. $4, 12x, 6$ **2.** $x, 5x^3, x^2$ **3.** $x^4, -6x^2, x^3$ **4.** $4x, 6x, 8x$

Solve each equation by cross multiplying.

5. $\frac{5}{x} = \frac{10}{3}$ **6.** $\frac{1}{3x+3} = \frac{1}{x+4}$ **7.** $\frac{3}{x+9} = \frac{x}{x-3}$ **8.** $\frac{2}{x+2} = \frac{3}{x+3}$

Solve each equation.

9. $\frac{1}{3} + \frac{2}{x} = \frac{5}{6}$ **10.** $x + 10 = \frac{-25}{x}$ **11.** $\frac{2}{(x-3)^2} = 1 - \frac{1}{x-3}$

12. $\frac{36}{x} = -12 - x$ **13.** $\frac{1}{x-4} + \frac{1}{x+4} = \frac{16}{x^2-16}$ **14.** $\frac{7}{3x-12} - \frac{1}{x-4} = \frac{4}{3}$

Literal equations

A literal equation is an equation that contains more than one letter as a variable. In a literal equation, any one of the letters can be expressed in terms of the others.

Solve $mx + n = y$ for x

$mx + n - n = y - n$ Subtract n from both sides of equation.

$mx = y - n$ Divide by m on both sides of equation.

$x = \dfrac{y - n}{m}$ Simplify to solve for x.

Solve $P = 2\ell + 2w$ for w, where P is the perimeter of a rectangle, ℓ is the length, and w is the width.

$P - 2\ell = 2\ell - 2\ell + 2w$ Subtract 2ℓ from both sides of equations.

$\dfrac{P - 2\ell}{2} = \dfrac{2w}{2}$ Simplify and divide by 2 on both sides.

$\dfrac{P - 2\ell}{2} = w$ Solve for w.

Now, use this result to find the width of a rectangle whose length is 16m and whose perimeter is 56m.

$w = \dfrac{P - 2\ell}{2}$ Formula for width

$w = \dfrac{56 - 2(16)}{2}$ Substitute in values for the variables.

$w = \dfrac{56 - 32}{2}$ Simplify.

$w = 12m$ Solve for x.

Thus, the width of the rectangle using this literal equation is 12m.

Solve for x in each equation.

1. $c = 5x$

2. $x + 3y = z$

3. $-7x + y = -4x - 11y$

4. $z - xy - wx$

5. $x - y = z$

6. $-xy = z$

7. $kx - 2bc = 5y + 2$

8. $a = bx + c$

9. The formula for the perimeter of a rectangle is $P = 2\ell + 2w$. Solve for ℓ. Then find ℓ if the perimeter is 84 in., and the width is 18 in.

10. Give an example of a literal equation. Give a step-by-step description of how to solve it.

Problem solving using ratios and proportions

Ratios and proportions are used to solve many different types of word problems.
When setting up a proportion to solve a word problem, make sure the unit in both
numerators is the same and the unit in both denominators is the same.

A recipe for making cookies calls for 1,200g of flour to make 40 cookies.
How many cookies can be made using 900g of flour?

$$\frac{\text{flour}}{\text{cookies}} = \frac{\text{flour}}{\text{cookies}}$$ First, set up your units.

$$\frac{1,200g}{40 \text{ cookies}} = \frac{900g}{x}$$ Put your values in proportion and place an x for the unknown value.

$$1,200x = 900(40)$$ Cross multiply.

$$x = 30 \text{ cookies}$$ Solve for x.

Thus, if we used 900g of flour, we would make 30 cookies.

Solve each problem.

1. Find the measures of two supplementary angles if their measures are in a ratio of 5:4.
   (Hint: Supplementary angles have a sum of 180°.)

2. Mr. Taylor drove 360 miles and used 12 gallons of gas. How far can he drive on a full tank of
   20 gallons of gas?

3. The perimeter of a rectangle is 140 inches. The sides are in the ratio of 3:4. Find the area of
   the rectangle.

4. A recipe for baking blueberry muffins calls for 2 eggs for every dozen muffins. How many
   eggs would we need if we are going to bake 6 dozen muffins?

5. Find the measures of two complementary angles if their measures are in a ratio of 2:3.
   (Hint: Complementary angles have a sum of 90°.)

6. The area of a rectangle is 216 in.² The sides are in a ratio of 3:8. Find the perimeter of
   the rectangle.

Problem solving with work problems

A formula to remember when solving work problems is:

Time • rate = part of work completed: $w = r \cdot t$

Joe and Bob are going to paint Bob's house. Joe takes 5 days to paint a house, and Bob takes 7 days to paint the very same house. If they work together, how long will it take them to paint Bob's house?

First, set up the plan.

Let x = the number of days Joe and Bob work together.

Joe's part of the job done in one day = $\frac{1}{5}$

Bob's part of the job done in one day = $\frac{1}{7}$

Joe's part of the job completed = $\frac{1}{5}x$ or $\frac{x}{5}$

Bob's part of the job completed = $\frac{1}{7}x$ or $\frac{x}{7}$

Joe's part + Bob's part = whole job

Now, plug the values into the equation and solve for x.

$\frac{x}{5} + \frac{x}{7} = 1$

$35(\frac{x}{5} + \frac{x}{7}) = 1(35)$ Multiply by the common denominator.

$7x + 5x = 35$ Simplify.

$12x = 35$ Divide by 12.

$x = 2\frac{11}{12}$ days   Solve for x.

Thus, if Joe and Bob work together, they can have Bob's house painted in $2\frac{11}{12}$ days.

Solve each problem.

1. Stacey can type a document in 6 hours. What part can she type in 2 hours? in n hours?

2. John can bike to his grandma's house in 1 hour. What part of the route can he bike in 45 minutes?

3. Jane takes 12 hours to clean her dad's office building. Lisa has cleaned it in 14 hours. How long would it take the girls if they cleaned it together?

4. It takes Matt 10 hours to wallpaper a bathroom. Dan has done the same bathroom in 8 hours. How long would it take if the boys wallpapered it together?

5. Ashley and Will can paint their bedroom in 5 hours if they work together. If it takes Ashley 9 hours to paint it alone, how long would it take Will to paint it alone?

6. It takes Heather 22 hours to wallpaper two rooms. She and Jill can do it together in 16 hours. How long would it take Jill to wallpaper alone?

Review of Unit 12

Topics Covered:
- Ratios and Proportions   Problem Solving Using Ratios and Proportions
- Rational Equations   Problem Solving with Work Problems
- Literal Equations

1. Give the definition of a ratio. Give an example.

2. Give the definition of a proportion. Give an example.

3. Give an example of a literal equation and describe step-by-step how to solve it.

4. Find the least common multiple in the set $3x^2$, $5x^3$, $6x$.

5. Identify the extremes and the means in $\frac{x+2}{x} = \frac{9}{x^2}$.

Solve.

6. $\frac{x}{5} = \frac{6}{2}$

7. $\frac{1}{4x-1} = \frac{1}{3x+5}$

8. $\frac{3}{4} + \frac{3}{x} = \frac{5}{8}$

9. $\frac{9}{x} = \frac{7}{x+2}$

10. $x + 5 = \frac{-4}{x}$

11. $\frac{-25}{x^2} = \frac{10}{x} + 1$

12. $\frac{x+1}{x+2} = \frac{3}{2}$

13. $\frac{8}{4x+16} - \frac{1}{x+4} = \frac{3}{4}$

14. $\frac{2}{x-3} + \frac{2}{x+3} = \frac{24}{x^2-9}$

15. Solve $P = 2\ell + 2w$ for w, where P is the perimeter, ℓ is the length, and w is the width. Then given $P = 96$ in. and $\ell = 25$ in., find the width.

16. When Grandma bakes cookies, she uses 1500g of flour for 5 dozen cookies. How much flour would she need it she were only baking 3 dozen cookies?

17. If they work together, Rose and Jeff can winterize and close the swimming pool in 5 hours. If it takes Rose 9 hours to close the pool by herself, how long would it take Jeff to do it by himself?

18. Show with an example what the extremes and means are in a proportion.

19. Give two examples of when a proportion can be used to solve a work problem.

Unit 12 Test

Applying Rational Equations and Proportions

1. What is the difference between a ratio and a proportion? Give an example of each.

2. Identify the extremes and means in the proportion $\frac{4x}{7} = \frac{6}{11}$.

3. What are the steps to solving a rational equation? Give an example and show step-by-step how to solve it.

4. What is a literal equation?

5. Find the least common multiple in the set $x^2 - 9$, x, $x + 3$.

Solve each equation by cross multiplying.

6. $\frac{x}{12} = \frac{5}{3}$

7. $\frac{x-2}{x} = \frac{3}{4}$

8. $\frac{x}{5} = \frac{x}{x-1}$

Solve each equation by finding the LCD.

9. $\frac{x}{x-2} = \frac{4}{x+3} + 1$

10. $\frac{x}{x-2} = \frac{1}{x} + \frac{4}{x^2-2x}$

11. $\frac{2}{6-x} + \frac{3}{x+4} = \frac{5}{x^2-2x-24}$

12. If 3 out of 5 people own a DVD player, how many people own one in a population of 10,000 people?

13. Toby and her sister can clean their house together in 7 hours. It takes Toby twice as long as her sister to clean alone. How long would it take each of them to clean the house alone?

14. Solve $ax + bx = z$ for x. Then solve the same equation for b.

15. The area of a rectangle is 640 m². The sides are in a ratio of 5:8. Find the perimeter of the rectangle.

16. Find the measures of two supplementary angles if their measures are in a ratio of 2:7. (Remember: Supplementary angles have a sum of 180°.)

Answer Key

Page 5
1. X; **2.** expression; **3.** X; **4.** X; **5.** expression;
6. X; **7.** expression; **8.** expression; **9.** 11; **10.** 3;
11. 5; **12.** 24; **13.** 15; **14.** 21; **15.** 13; **16.** 34;
17. 84; **18.** $r + 9$; **19.** $20b$; **20.** $2t$; **21.** $2/3c$;
22. $y - 9$; **23.** $3x \div 10$

Page 6
1. multiplication; **2.** parentheses $(10 + 4)$;
3. subtraction; **4.** division; **5.** division;
6. division; **7.** multiplication; **8.** innermost
parentheses $(12 - 7)$; **9.** 35; **10.** 28; **11.** 13;
12. 2; **13.** 22; **14.** 43; **15.** 28; **16.** 20; **17.** 11;
18. 6; **19.** 22; **20.** 67

Page 7
1. 3^6; **2.** a^2b^3; **3.** 9^2; **4.** x^3y; **5.** 10^5; **6.** 4^55^4; **7.** 8;
8. 915; **9.** 36; **10.** 10; **11.** 98; **12.** 21; **13.** 375;
14. 1,000; **15.** 72; **16.** 155; **17.** 20; **18.** 14;
19. 1,010; **20.** 28

Page 8
1. 48 ft.; **2.** 80 cm; **3.** 28 in.; **4.** 72 mm; **5.** 36 in.;
6. 44 cm; **7.** 14 in.^{2}; **8.** 169 mm^2; **9.** 14.7 yd.^{2};
10. 36 cm^2; **11.** 50 ft.^{2}; **12.** 11.56 in.^{2}; **13.** 45 ft.^{2};
14. 192 cm^2; **15.** 30 mm^2

Page 9
1. commutative property of addition;
2. associative property of multiplication;
3. associative property of addition;
4. commutative property of addition;
5. commutative property of multiplication;
6. commutative property of multiplication;
7. not circled; **8.** circled; **9.** circled; **10.** not
circled; **11.** $12a$; **12.** $56n$; **13.** $80t$; **14.** $24r$;
15. $10x$; **16.** $90k$; **17.** txy; **18.** $efgh$

Page 10
1. $4(8 + 9 + 2)$; **2.** $(6 + 5 - 9)7$; **3.** $(8 - 5)a$;
4. $8(3 - 7)$; **5.** $x(3 + 4 + 10)$; **6.** $k(t + r + s)$; **7.** $9 \cdot 8 + 9 \cdot 7$, 135; **8.** $10 \cdot 7 - 10 \cdot 3$, 40; **9.** $2x \cdot 6 - 3y \cdot 6$, $12x - 18y$; **10.** $5 \cdot 6y - 5 \cdot 12$, $30y - 60$; **11.** $12 \cdot 3 - 5 \cdot 3$, 21; **12.** $10 \cdot 2 + 12 \cdot 2 + 14 \cdot 2$, 72; **13.** $10 \cdot x - 10 \cdot y - 10 \cdot z$, $10x - 10y - 10z$; **14.** $x \cdot 7 - 2z \cdot 7$, $7x - 14z$; **15.** $12a + 20b + 24c + 32d + 8e + 4f$; **16.** $120w - 20x - 90y + 60z$; **17.–18.** Answers will vary.

Page 11
1. $7c$, $12c$; **2.** none; **3.** none; **4.** $5r$, $-10r$; **5.** $5t$, $7t$; **6.** q, $2q$, $5q$; **7.** $5m$; **8.** $23y$; **9.** $31s - 8$;
10. already simplified; **11.** $18q + 14$; **12.** already
simplified; **13.** $2a$; **14.** $5t + 4m$; **15.** $21w + 8$;
16. $38a + 14$, 204; **17.** $8b + 31$, 95

Page 12
1. true; **2.** true; **3.** false; **4.** true; **5.** yes; **6.** no;
7. no; **8.** yes; **9.** no; **10.** yes; **11.** yes; **12.** no;
13. {0, 1, 2, 3}; **14.** {2}; **15.** {0, 1, 2, 3, 4};
16. {6}; **17.** {2, 4, 6, 8}; **18.** {4, 6, 8}

Page 13
1. parentheses (work inside out); **2.** exponents;
3. multiplication/division from left to right;
4. addition/subtraction from left to right;
5. equation; **6.** expression; **7.** inequality;
8. inequality; **9.** 30m^2; **10.** 144 in.^{2}; **11.** 2;
12. 108; **13.** 38; **14.** 26 in.; **15.** commutative;
16. distributive; **17.** distributive; **18.** commutative;
19. associative; **20.** associative; **21.** $30t$;

Page 14
22. $7a - 7b + 35$; **23.** $14y$; **24.** $72n$;
25. $9k - 12$; **26.** $9t + m$; **27.** {5}; **28.** {0, 1, 3}

Page 14
1. $10 - y$; **2.** $3s$; **3.** $r + 11$; **4.** $t + 11$; **5.** 3; **6.** 5;
7. 6; **8.** $2x + 11y$; **9.** 14; **10.** 30; **11.** 15; **12.** 11;
13. $28m^2$; **14.** 17; **15.** 44 in.; **16.–21.** Examples
will vary.; **22.** {10}; **23.** {0, 5, 10}; **24.** {5, 10}

Page 15
1. 3 1/2; **2.** 0; **3.** -3; **4.** 1 1/2; **5.** -1; **6.** -4 1/2;
7. 2 1/2; **8.** -2;
9.–14.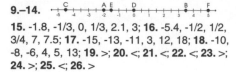
15. -1.8, -1/3, 0, 1/3, 2.1, 3; **16.** -5.4, -1/2, 1/2,
3/4, 7, 7.5; **17.** -15, -13, -11, 3, 12, 18; **18.** -10,
-8, -6, 4, 5, 13; **19.** >; **20.** <; **21.** <; **22.** <; **23.** >;
24. >; **25.** <; **26.** >

Page 16
1. -5; **2.** 2.6; **3.** 3/4; **4.** 0; **5.** 40; **6.** -2.8; **7.** 12;
8. -8; **9.** $89.25; **10.** -75; **11.** 10; **12.** -23; **13.** 0;
14. 42; **15.** =; **16.** >; **17.** <; **18.** -15; **19.** 20;
20. -12; **21.** -5; **22.** 16; **23.** 0

Page 17
1. Start at 7 and move 8 places to the right.
Result is 15.; **2.** Start at -5 and move 9 places
to the right. Result is 4.; **3.** Start at 10 and
move 7 places to the left. Result is 3.; **4.** Start
at -11 and move 6 places to the left. Result is
-17.; **5.** 13; **6.** -6; **7.** -13; **8.** 21; **9.** -5; **10.** -5;
11. 0; **12.** 8; **13.** -5; **14.** -11; **15.** -4; **16.** 9

Page 18
1. 7; **2.** -8; **3.** 22; **4.** 23; **5.** -21; **6.** 13; **7.** 3; **8.** 8;
9. -4; **10.** -1; **11.** 0; **12.** 11; **13.** -25; **14.** -44;
15. -1; **16.** $-5 + 8$, 3 yd. gain; **17.** $-8 + 5 - 4$, net
loss of 7 pounds

Page 19
1. $7 + -9$; **2.** $-6 + 4$; **3.** $-11 + -5$; **4.** $12 + 15$;
5. $8 + -3$; **6.** $22 + -5$; **7.** $4 + -11$; **8.** $-4 + 9$; **9.** -2;
10. 12; **11.** -9; **12.** 12; **13.** 0; **14.** -13; **15.** 8;
16. -6; **17.** 3; **18.** -3; **19.** -14; **20.** 17

Page 20
1. negative; **2.** negative; **3.** positive; **4.** negative;
5. positive; **6.** positive; **7.** negative; **8.** positive;
9. -24; **10.** -12; **11.** -1; **12.** 0; **13.** 15; **14.** 8;
15. 36; **16.** -49; **17.** 15; **18.** 0; **19.** -75; **20.** 0

Page 21
1. 1/2; **2.** 1; **3.** none; **4.** -9; **5.** -4; **6.** 3/4; **7.** -1/8;
8. 1/10; **9.** 3; **10.** -4; **11.** undefined; **12.** -7, **13.** -9;
14. 1; **15.** -4; **16.** 0; **17.** 25; **18.** -14; **19.** 1; **20.** -9

Page 22
1. -39; **2.** -58; **3.** 35; **4.** -33; **5.** 98; **6.** 38; **7.** -69;
8. -71; **9.** -16; **10.** 7; **11.** -210; **12.** -2; **13.** 36; **14.** -2

Page 23
1. $18y$; **2.** $-18b$; **3.** $6t$; **4.** $2x$; **5.** $-5c$; **6.** $-16d + 17w$; **7.** $-2a$; **8.** 0; **9.** $-5a + b$; **10.** $P = 2(3x) + 2(x + y)$, $P = 8x + 2y$; **11.** $P = 2(3y + 4x) + 2(x - 2y)$, $P = 10x + 2y$; **12.** $P = 2(6x - y + 3) + 2(5x + 3y - 4)$, $P = 22x + 4y - 2$

Page 24
1. $-24x - 16$; **2.** $-12y - 33$; **3.** $2t - 7$; **4.** $-16y + 32$; **5.** $-s - 5$; **6.** $-3b - 2$; **7.** $a - b + 2$; **8.** $60d - 30$; **9.** $-21z + 16$; **10.** $-x - 1$, -5; **11.** $-5z - 1$, 9;
12. $-4y - 5$, -1; **13.** $8a + 6$, -34

Page 25
1. A rate is the comparison of two quantities
measured in different units. A ratio is the
comparison of two quantities measured in the
same units.; **2.** rate, miles/hour; **3.** ratio,
area/area; **4.** rate, dollars/hour; **5.** ratio, price
of scoop/price of container; **6.** 29.5 miles/gallon;
7. $5.25 per hour; **8.** 70 miles per hour; **9.** $4.\overline{6}$
was the average score per hole.

Page 26
1.–5.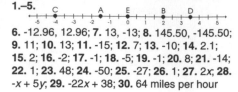
6. -12.96, 12.96; **7.** 13, -13; **8.** 145.50, -145.50;
9. 11; **10.** 13; **11.** -15; **12.** 7; **13.** -10; **14.** 2.1;
15. 2; **16.** -2; **17.** -1; **18.** -5; **19.** -1; **20.** 8; **21.** -14;
22. 1; **23.** 48; **24.** -50; **25.** -27; **26.** 1; **27.** $2x$; **28.** $-x + 5y$; **29.** $-22x + 38$; **30.** 64 miles per hour

Page 27
1. -4, -1/3, 0, 2, 5; **2.** -7, -2, 1/2, 2, 7; **3.** -12, -3 1/2,
5, 6, 11; **4.** -4 1/2, 4 1/2; **5.** -2, 2; **6.** 5, -5; **7.** 1 1/2,
-1 1/2; **8.** 0, 0; **9.–10.** Examples will vary.; **11.** =;
12. <; **13.** >; **14.** -4; **15.** 0; **16.** 3; **17.** -2; **18.** -6;
19. -2; **20.** undefined; **21.** 12; **22.** -6; **23.** -1;
24. 33; **25.** -15; **26.** -5; **27.** A rate is a
comparison of two measurements with
different units. A ratio is a comparison of two
measurements with the same units. Examples
will vary.

Page 28
1. $Ax + By = C$; **2.** yes; **3.** yes; **4.** no; **5.** no;
6. yes; **7.** yes; **8.** $-6x - 3y = 11$; **9.** $2x - 4y = 14$;
10. $7x + 3y = 5$; **11.** $3x - y = -8$; **12.** $8x + 10y = 9$; **13.** $-10x - 7y = -11$; **14.** $2x + 7y = 12$; **15.** $x + y = -15$

Page 29
1. $y = mx + b$; **2.** $m = 2$, $b = 5$; **3.** $m = 1$, $b = -10$;
4. $m = -1$, $b = 4$; **5.** $m = -3$, $b = 7$; **6.** $m = -5$, $b = 0$;
7. $m = 0$, $b = 5$; **8.** $y = -3x + 10$; **9.** $y = 7x + 12$;
10. $y = -7x + 5$; **11.** $y = -x - 4$; **12.** $y = x + 2$;
13. $y = -1/2x + 8$; **14.** $y = 1/4x - 1$; **15.** $y = -2x - 1$

Page 30
1. $y - y_1 = m(x - x_1)$; **2.** no; **3.** no; **4.** yes; **5.** yes;
6. yes; **7.** no; **8.** $y - 3 = 4(x - 2)$; **9.** $y + 4 = -8(x + 5)$; **10.** $y - 7 = -3(x + 5)$; **11.** $y - 4 = -(x - 2)$;
12. $y - 2 = x + 1$; **13.** $y + 8 = 2(x - 6)$; **14.** $y + 1 = 1/2(x - 1)$; **15.** $y + 1 = -1/2(x + 4)$

Page 31
1. $m = -2$, $b = 5$; **2.** $m = -8$, $b = 0$; **3.** $m = -1$,
$b = -2$; **4.** $m = 1$, $b = 9$; **5.** $m = 0$, $b = 7$; **6.** $m = 2$, $b = -7$; **7.** $m = 4$, $b = 6$; **8.** $m = -1$, $b = 0$;
9. $y = 4x - 1$; **10.** $y = 7$; **11.** $y = -2x - 5$;
12. $y = -1/4x - 3$; **13.** $y = 1/2x - 6$; **14.** $y = -x + 8$; **15.** $y = x + 2$; **16.** $y = 4x$; **17.** slope-intercept
form; **18.** y-intercept

Page 32
1. -1; **2.** 10; **3.** -6; **4.** 9; **5.** 13; **6.** -11; **7.** 19; **8.** 1;
9. -6; **10.** -11; **11.** 15; **12.** 10; **13.** $y = 3x + 19$;
14. $y = 4x + 1$; **15.** $y = -x - 6$; **16.** $y = -2x - 11$;
17. $y = -3x + 15$; **18.** $y = -3x + 10$; **19.** $y = 2/3x + 3$; **20.** $y = -2x + 2$

Answer Key

Page 33
1. 3; **2.** -2/3; **3.** -2; **4.** 2; **5.** 1; **6.** 0; **7.** $y = 3x + 2$;
8. $y = -2/3x + 3$; **9.** $y = -2x + 7$; **10.** $y = 2x$;
11. $y = x - 3$; **12.** $y = 8$; **13.** $y = -x - 6$; **14.** $y = 1$;
15. $y = -2x + 2$

Page 34
1. $Ax + By = C$; **2.** $y = mx + b$; **3.** $y - y_1 = m(x - x_1)$;
4. You need the value of the slope and its
y-intercept.; **5.–6.** Explanations will vary.
5. Substitute the slope's value for m and the
point's x value for x_1 and the point's y value for
y_1 in the equation $y_1 = mx_1 + b$. Solve for b.
Substitute the m and b values into the
equation $y = mx + b$; **6.** Substitute the two
points into the equation $m = \frac{y_2 - y_1}{x_2 - x_1}$, then use
one of the two points and, combined with the
slope, solve using same steps as in answer 5.;
7. $y - 9 = 8(x - 6)$ or $y + 7 = 8(x - 4)$; **8.** $y + 5 = 4(x + 3)$ or $y + 1 = 4(x + 2)$; **9.** $y - 6 = x - 7$ or
$y - 2 = x - 3$; **10.** $y = -8x + 18$, y-int. = 18;
11. $y = -x - 7$, y-int. = -7; **12.** $y = 7x + 37$, y-int.
= 37; **13.** $y = x + 3$, slope = 1, y-int. = 3; **14.** $y = -2x + 6$, slope = -2, y-int. = 6; **15.** $y = 7x + 4$,
slope = 7, y-int. = 4

Page 35
1. standard; **2.** slope-intercept; **3.** point-slope;
4. the slope and the y-intercept values; **5.** You
need 2 points on the line, $\frac{rise}{run}$ or $\frac{y_2 - y_1}{x_2 - x_1}$ to find
the slope. Take the difference of the y
coordinates divided by the difference of the x
coordinates.; **6.** $m = 2$, $b = -5$; **7.** $m = -3$, $b = -2$;
8. $m = -5$, $b = 12$; **9.** $y = -4x + 19$, y-int. = 19;
10. $y = 4x - 26$, y-int. = -26; **11.** $y = -2x + 3$, y-int. = 3; **12.** $y = -2x - 8$, y-int. = -8; **13.** $y = -3x + 5$, y-int. = 5; **14.** $y = 5x + 28$, y-int. = 28; **15.** $y + 2 = -2(x - 8)$, $m = -2$, $b = 14$ or $y + 10 = -2(x - 12)$; **16.** $y - 4 = -(x + 6)$, $m = -1$, $b = -2$ or $y + 7 = -(x - 5)$; **17.** $y - 2 = 2(x + 1)$, $m = 2$, $b = 4$ or
$y + 2(x + 3)$

Page 36
1. $x = 33$; **2.** $x = -17$; **3.** $x = -7$; **4.** $x = -7$; **5.** $x = -1$;
6. $x = 0$; **7.** $x = 9$; **8.** $x = 0$; **9.** $x = -14$; **10.** $x = 3$;
11. $x = -19$; **12.** $x = -3$; **13.** $x + 10 = 38$, $x = 28$;
14. $x - 40 = 90$, $130

Page 37
1. $x = 7$; **2.** $x = -6$; **3.** $x = -7$; **4.** $x = -18$; **5.** $x = 4$;
6. $x = -16$; **7.** $x = -8$; **8.** $x = 12$; **9.** $x = -20$;
10. $x = -12$; **11.** $x = -15$; **12.** $x = -4$; **13.** $21 = 3x$,
$x = 7$, Mary worked 7 hours.; **14.** $8x = -96$, -12
is the number; **15.** $2/3x = 80$, $x = 120$, John's
savings before he bought the radio is $120

Page 38
1. $x = 4$; **2.** $x = -28$; **3.** $x = 10$; **4.** $x = -10$;
5. $x = 12$; **6.** $x = -20$; **7.** $x = -2$; **8.** $x = 3$; **9.** $x = -4$;
10. $x = -1$; **11.** $x = 18$; **12.** $x = -2$; **13.** $32 = 3n - 7$, $n = 13$; **14.** $-25 = 4n + 7$, $n = -8$; **15.** $2x - 12 = 270$, $x = 141$ lbs.

Page 39
1. $x = 2$; **2.** $x = -4$; **3.** $x = -6$; **4.** $x = -3$; **5.** $x = -2$;
6. $x = 2$; **7.** $x = -2$; **8.** $x = -1/2$; **9.** $x = -6$; **10.** $2p = p + 45$, $p = 45; **11.** $n - 12 = 3n$, $n = -6$;
12. $t + 65 = 5t - 15$, $t = 20°$

Page 40
1. $15x - 30$; **2.** $-12x - 10$; **3.** $-4x + 24 = 14 - 14x$;
4. $-10 + 25x$; **5.** $-48 - 28x$; **6.** $-72x + 32 = -18x - 27$; **7.** $x = 3$; **8.** $x = 2$; **9.** $x = 24$; **10.** $x = -8$;
11. $x = 5$; **12.** $x = -1$; **13.** $4(n + 7) = n - 44$,
$n = -24$; **14.** $n + 16 = 8(n + 9)$, $n = -8$

Page 41
1. 60 mi./hr.; **2.** 600 tickets; **3.** $3.50; **4.** $950;
5. $175

Page 42
1. $x = 5$; **2.** $x = -15$; **3.** $x = -1$; **4.** $x = 13$; **5.** $x = 1$;
6. $x = -4$; **7.** $x = -4$; **8.** $x = -2$; **9.** $3(a - 12) = 24$,
age = 20 years; **10.** $6a + 10 = 4a + 40$, $a = 15$
years; **11.** 585 miles; **12.** 200 tickets

Page 43
1. $x = 27$; **2.** $x = 4$; **3.** $x = -7$; **4.** $x = 4$; **5.** $x = -33$;
6. $x = -2$; **7.** $x = 1$; **8.** $x = -15$; **9.** $2t - 5 = 21$, $t = 13°F$; **10.** $3s = s + 110$, $s = 55; **11.** $4n - 9 + 12 = 2n - 5$, $n = -4$; **12.** $350 = r \cdot 5$, $r = 70$
mi./hr.; **13.** $n = 200$ tickets

Page 44
1. B; **2.** D; **3.** C; **4.** A;

5.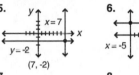
(7, -2)

6.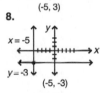
(-5, 3)

7.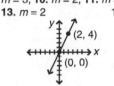
(1, -1)

8.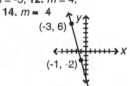
(-5, -3)

9. no; **10.** yes; **11.** yes; **12.** no;

13.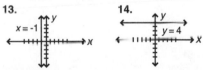

14.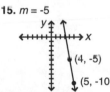

Page 45
1. no; **2.** yes; **3.** yes; **4.** no; **5.–8.** Solutions will
vary. **5.** $y = x + 5$; **6.** $y = 2x + 7$; **7.** $y = 3/4x - 3$;
8. $y = 5/3x + -5$;

9.
(-6, 0) (0, -8)

10.
(0, 1) (1, -2)

11.
(1, -3) (0, -5)

12.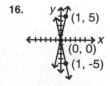
(-3, 0) (0, -2)

Page 46
1. x-int. = 4, y-int. = 3; **2.** x-int. = 5, y-int. = -2;
3. x-int. = -3, y-int. = 1; **4.** x-int. = -4, y-int. = -6;

5.
(5, 0) (0, -2)

6.
(0, 3) (-1, 0)

7.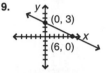
(-4, 0) (0, -3)

8.
(0, 4) (2, 0)

9.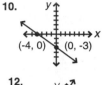
(0, 3) (6, 0)

10.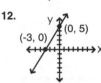
(-4, 0) (0, -3)

11.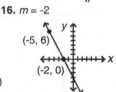
(4, 0) (0, -9)

12.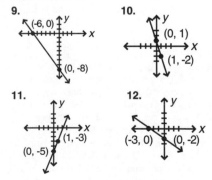
(-3, 0) (0, 5)

Page 47
1. rises from left to right; **2.** falls from left to right;
3. rises from left to right; **4.** vertical; **5.** horizontal;
6. falls from left to right; **7.** $m = 5$; **8.** $m = -1$; **9.**
$m = 3$; **10.** $m = 2$; **11.** $m = -5$; **12.** $m = 4$;
13. $m = 2$ **14.** $m = 4$

(2, 4) (0, 0)   (-3, 6) (-1, -2)

15. $m = -5$ **16.** $m = -2$

(4, -5) (5, -10)   (-5, 6) (-2, 0)

Page 48
1. $y = 7/4x$; **2.** $y = -18$; **3.** $y = 3/2x + 6$; **4.** $y = 8x + 4$; **5.** $y = -4/5x - 8$; **6.** $y = -7/2x - 5$; **7.** $m = -3$,
$b = 5$; **8.** $m = 7$, $b = 11$; **9.** $m = 2$, $b = -2$; **10.** $m = 4$, $b = -2$; **11.** $m = 1$, $b = -5$; **12.** $m = 1$, $b = 9$;
13. $y = -2x + 4$, $m = -2$, y-int. = 4, x-int. = 2; $y = -2x - 3$, $m = -2$, y-int. = -3, x-int. = -3/2; **14.** $y = x + 1$, $m = 1$, y-int. = 1, x-int. = -1; $y = -x + 1$, $m = -1$, y-int. = 1, x-int. = 1; **15.** $y = 3x + 3$, $m = 3$,
y-int. = 3, x-int. = -1; $y = -3x - 3$, $m = -3$, y-int. = -3, x-int. = -1; **16.** $y = 5x$, $m = 5$, y-int. = 0, x-int. = 0; $y = -5x$, $m = -5$, y-int. = 0, x-int. = 0;

13. (0, 4) (1, 2) (-1, -1) (0, -3)   **14.** (0, 1) (1, 2) (1, 0)

15. (1, 6) (0, 3) (0, -3) (1, -6)   **16.** (1, 5) (0, 0) (1, -5)

Answer Key

Page 49

1. (5, -2) 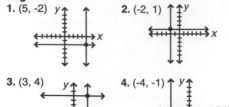 **2.** (-2, 1)

3. (3, 4) 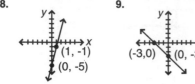 **4.** (-4, -1)

5. no; **6.** yes; **7.** no; **8.–11.** Solutions will vary.

8. 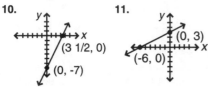 **9.**

10. 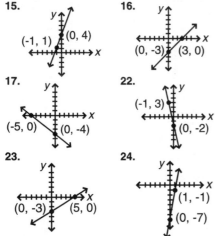 **11.**

12. $m = -1$, falls from left to right; **13.** $m = -4$, falls from left to right; **14.** $m = 1$, rises from left to right; **15.** $y = 3x + 4$, $m = 3$, y-int. = 4; **16.** $y = x - 3$, m = 1, y-int. = -3; **17.** $y = -4/5x - 4$, $m = -4/5$, y-int. = -4; **18.** x-int. = -5, y-int. = 5; **19.** x-int. = 7, y-int. = -3; **20.** x-int. = 8, y-int. = -5; **21.** x-int. = -15, y-int. = -5. **22.–24.** Methods will vary.

15. 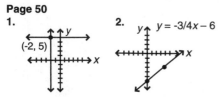 **16.**

17. **22.**

23. **24.**

Page 50

1. **2.** $y = -3/4x - 6$

3. $x = 7$, Answers will vary.; **4.** No, because $-3(4) - (-2) \neq 10$, $-10 \neq 10$; **5.** x-int. = -1/2, y-int. = -3; **6.** x-int. = -2, y-int. = 5; **7.** x-int. = -4, y-int. = 8; **8.** $m = 0$, horizontal; **9.** $m = 4$, rises from left to right; **10.** m is undefined, vertical; **11.** $y = 7x - 1$, $m = 7$, y-int. = -1; **12.** $y = -x + 5$, $m = -1$, y-int. = 5; **13.** $y = -2x + 4$, $m = -2$, y-int. = 4;

14.–16. Methods and explanations will vary.

5. 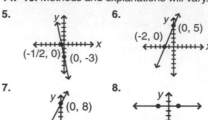 **6.**

7. 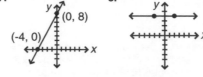 **8.**

9. 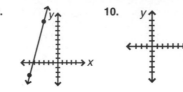 **10.**

11. 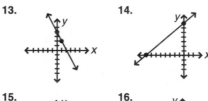 **12.**

13. 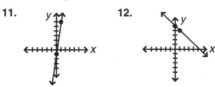 **14.**

15. 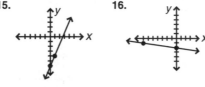 **16.**

Page 51

1. m = Sherri's matches won, $m + 4$ = Mary's matches won; **2.** s = John's stickers, $7s - 3$ = Joey's stickers; **3.** ℓ = length of second board, $2\ell + 2$ = length of first board; **4.** p = price of football ticket last year, $p + 1/3$ price of football ticket this year; **5.** d = dollars Sarah raised, $4d - 75$ = dollars Kent raised; **6.** blue pens; **7.** $n - 8$; **8.** n

Page 52

1. mom's age = $3y - 7$, Steve's age = y; $y + (3y - 7) = 65$; Steve is 18 years old. Steve's mom is 47 years old.; **2.** T = Tim's score, $T + 8$ = Brianne's score; $T + (T + 8) = 96$; Tim's score is 44. Brianne's score is 52. **3.** n = smaller number, $8n$ = larger number; $8n - n = 42$; Smaller number is 6. Larger number is 48.; **4.** J = Julie's hours, $J + 12$ = Shelley's hours; $J + (J + 12) = 72$; Julie worked 30 hours. Shelley worked 42 hours.; **5.** p = people in second group, $3p - 8$ = people in first group; $p + (3p - 8) = 80$; There are 58 people in the first group and 22 people in the second group.; **6.** Kevin's cards = c, Jake's cards = $3c - 20$; $c + 3c - 20 = 1,240$; Kevin has 315 cards. Jake has 925 cards.

Page 53

1. $2(4x) + 2(4x - 2) = 12$, length = 4 in., width = 2 in.; **2.** $3(2x - 3) = 33$, side = 11 in.; **3.** $4(2x) = 56$, side = 14 in.; **4.** $2w + 2(4w) = 50$, width = 5 cm, length = 20 cm; **5.** $(s + 6) + s + (2s - 5) = 25$, 12 in., 6 in., 7 in.; **6.** $2(3b - 8) + b = 33$, base = 7 cm, leg = 13 cm, leg = 13 cm; **7.** $3(2x - 3) = 51$, side = 17 in.

Page 54

1. 42; **2.** 24; **3.** 90; **4.** 30; **5.** 33/4 = 8 1/4; **6.** 78; **7.** 46/9 = 5 1/9; **8.** 100/9 = 11 1/9; **9.** -3/4; **10.** -100/7 = -14 2/7; **11.** $1/2a + 8 = 24$, 32 years; **12.** $3/4n - 5 = 2n$, -4; **13.** 0; 14. 2

Page 55

1. 10^2; **2.** 10^3; **3.** 10^4; **4.** 0.3; **5.** 2.2; **6.** 4; **7.** -5.8; **8.** 179; **9.** 47.775; **10.** $n - 0.08n = 1.38$, 1.5; **11.** $n + 0.35n = 0.675$, 0.5

Page 56

1. 0.47, 47/100; **2.** 0.155, 31/200; **3.** 0.33, 33/100; **4.** 0.085, 17/200; **5.** 0.005, 1/200; **6.** 0.1275, 51/400; **7.** 35%; **8.** 50%; **9.** 1.5%; **10.** 60%; **11.** 150%; **12.** 37.5%; **13.** 16; **14.** 12 1/2%; **15.** 20%; **16.** 160; **17.** 112.5; **18.** 8.1; **19.** 25%; **20.** 40%

Page 57

1. original price $1000, discount $250; **2.** $27.81; **3.** $6,250; **4.** $12,500; **5.** $5,000; **6.** $440

Page 58

1. $n - 54 = 5n - 6$, n = -12; **2.** b = second part, $3b + 8$ = first part, $b + (3b + 8) = 56$; first part = 44 in., second part = 12 in.; **3.** $2w + 2(2w + 10) = 50$, length = 20 cm, width = 5 cm; **4.** 15/18 = 1 7/8; **5.** -1.86; **6.** 1/14; **7.** 0.47; **8.** 130; **9.** 48.1; **10.** 9 3/8%; **11.** $50

Page 59

1. 13/28; **2.** 17/26; **3.** 10.32; **4.** -1.91; **5.** x = second piece, $2x + 6$ = first piece; $x + 2x + 6 = 60$; first piece 42 in., second piece = 18 in.; **6.** x = side, $4x - 5$ = base; $2x + 4x - 5 = 67$, base = 43 m, side = 12 m, side = 12 m; **7.** ℓ = length, $2\ell + 12$ = width, $2\ell + 2(2\ell + 12) = 90$; length = 11 ft., width = 34 ft.; **8.** 7.2; **9.** 20%; **10.** 12 1/2%; **11.** $500; **12.** $5,500

Page 60

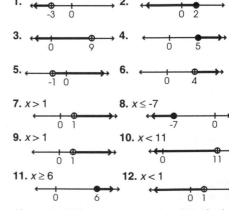

13. $y + 5 > 150$, $y > 145$; Don already rushed more than 145 yards.; **14.** $c - 24 > 50$, $c > 74$; Tara had more than 74 cookies.

Answer Key

Page 61
1. $x > 15$; **2.** $x < -6$; **3.** $x \leq 3$; **4.** $x \geq -3$; **5.** $x \leq -12$; **6.** $x < 7$; **7.** $x \geq -20$; **8.** $x > 0$; **9.** $x \leq -30$;
10. $x < 4$ **11.** $x \leq -3$
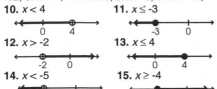
12. $x > -2$ **13.** $x \leq 4$
14. $x < -5$ **15.** $x \geq -4$
16. $3x > 132$, $x > 44$; **17.** $10x < 3.50$, $x < .35$; Each candy bar costs less than $\$.35$.

Page 62
1. $120 < x < 135$; **2.** $x = 250$ or $x > 250$; **3.** $x = 3$ or $x < 3$; **4.** $12 \leq x \leq 18$; **5.** $-5 \leq x \leq 3$; **6.** $x \geq 2$ or $x \leq -4$; **7.** $x < 2$ or $x > 4$; **8.** $2 \leq x \leq 3$; **9.** $-4 < x < 1$; **10.** $x < 2$ and $x > -7$, $-7 < x < 2$

Page 63
1. d; **2.** c; **3.** e; **4.** a; **5.** b;
6.   **7.** all real numbers
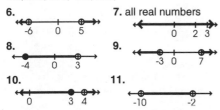
8.   **9.**
10.   **11.**

Page 64
1. no; **2.** yes; **3.** yes; **4.** no;
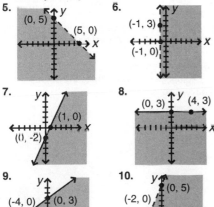
5. (0, 5) (5, 0)   **6.** (-1, 3) (-1, 0)
7. (1, 0) (0, -2)   **8.** (0, 3) (4, 3)
9. (-4, 0) (0, 3)   **10.** (-2, 0) (0, 5)

Page 65
1. (0, 5); **2.** (3, 0); **3.** (-1, -2); **4.** (-2, -2); **5.** (0, -4); **6.** (5, 7);
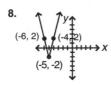
7. (-1, 3) (1, 3) (0, 0)   **8.** (-6, 2) (-4, 2) (-5, -2)

9. (0, 0) (-1, -7) (1, -7)   **10.** (0, 2) (1, 4) (2, 2)

11. (-5, 1) (-7, 1) (-6, 0)   **12.** (-3, 4) (-1, 4) (-2, -1)
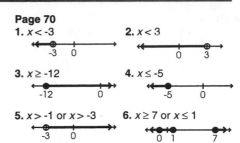

Page 66
1. $|8x - 3| = 6$; **2.** $|x + 2| = 1$; **3.** $|x - 16| = 24$; **4.** $|x - 6| = -5$; **5.** 6, -6; **6.** 3, 13; **7.** 3, -2; **8.** 9, -9; **9.** -7, -17; **10.** 3, -1; **11.** 7, -17; **12.** 3, -1; **13.** 9, -5; **14.** 8, -24

Page 67
1. $x > 7$ or $x < -7$; **2.** $-2 \leq x \leq 2$; **3.** $7 - 3x < -10$ or $7 - 3x > 10$; **4.** $-12 < x - 9 < 12$; **5.** $2x - 5 \leq -7$ or $2x - 5 \geq 7$; **6.** $-11 < 5 + 6x < 11$; **7.** $-3 < x < 9$; **8.** $-2 \leq x \leq 8$; **9.** $-4 \leq x \leq 3$; **10.** $x \leq -15$ or $x \geq 1$; **11.** $x < -3$ or $x > 5$; **12.** $5 < x < 11$;
13. $-10 < x < -8$ **14.** $x < -3$ or $x > 2$
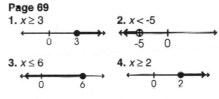
15. $x < -13$ or $x > -1$ **16.** $x \leq 2$ or $x \geq 3$
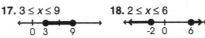
17. $3 \leq x \leq 9$ **18.** $2 \leq x \leq 6$
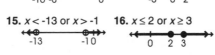

Page 68
1. $12n + 6 \leq 45$; **2.** $(4 + n)8 \geq 20$; **3.** $5n - 7 > 25$; **4.** $18 < 1/3a < 30$; **5.** $10 + 0.25m \leq 25$, $m \leq 60$, at most 60 miles; **6.** $(x + x + 2) \geq 36$, $x \geq 17$, $x + 2 \geq 19$; **7.** $15x \geq 300$, $x \geq 20$ stereos; **8.** $2.5x \leq 75$, $x \leq 30$ bricks

Page 69
1. $x \geq 3$ **2.** $x < -5$
3. $x \leq 6$ **4.** $x \geq 2$
5. $-12 < x < 2$ **6.** $4 \leq x \leq 6$
7. $x > 4$ or $x < 1$ **8.** $x \leq -1$ or $x \leq -5$
9. yes; **10.** no; **11.** (5, 7); **12.** (0, 10); **13.** (-4, -6)

14. (0, 5) (-6, 0)   **15.** (-3, 4) (-1, 4) (-2, -1)
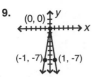
16. (0, -3) (1, -1)
17. -21, 3; **18.** 5, 1; **19.** $x \geq 4$ or $x \leq -2$; **20.** $-3 < x < 4$; **21.** $250 + 0.20 \leq 325$, 375 miles at most

Page 70
1. $x < -3$ **2.** $x < 3$
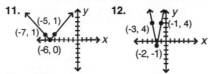
3. $x \geq -12$ **4.** $x \leq -5$
5. $x > -1$ or $x > -3$ **6.** $x \geq 7$ or $x \leq 1$

7. $-8 \leq x \leq 3$ **8.** $3 < x < 6$
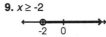
9. $x \geq -2$
10. (3, -2) is circled. **11.** (-1, 2) is circled.
12. (-2, -6) (-3, -5) (-1, -5)   **13.** (3, 4) (2, 2) (4, 2)
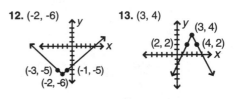
14. (0, 3) (-1, 2) (1, 2)   **15.** (-2, 0) (-3, 7) (-1, 7)
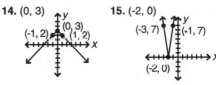
16. (-7, 0) (0, -4) (0, -6)   **17.** (2, 0)
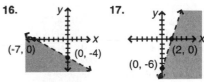
18. (-4, 0) (0, 5)
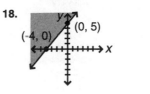
19. 3, -7; **20.** 4, -2; **21.** $-5 \leq x \leq 1$; **22.** $x \leq -2$ or $x \geq 4$; **23.** $x + (x + 2) + (x + 4) \leq 66$, $x \leq 20$, $x + 2 \leq 22$, $x + 4 \leq 24$

Page 71
1. yes; **2.** no; **3.** yes; **4.** (3, -2)   **5.** (2, -1)
(0, 2) (1 1/2, 0) (-1, -3) (3, -2); (3, 0) (0, -3) (2, -1) (0, -5)

Answer Key

6. (-1, -7)

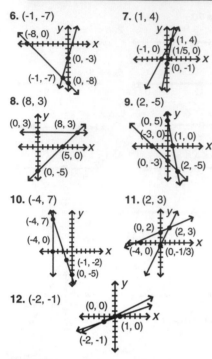

7. (1, 4)

8. (8, 3)

9. (2, -5)

10. (-4, 7)

11. (2, 3)

12. (-2, -1)

Page 72
1.–4. Answers will vary. Possible answers:
1. $y = -3x + 4$; **2.** $x = 5y + 10$; **3.** $y = -6x - 3$;
4. $x = -5y - 11$; **5.** (-1, -1); **6.** (-2, -5); **7.** (-7, 3);
8. (4, -2); **9.** (1, 1); **10.** (4, -5); **11.** (-3, 0);
12. (-4, 3); **13.** (3, 1)

Page 73
1. (3, 1/2); **2.** (1, 1); **3.** (-18/5, -10); **4.** (9/2, 2);
5. (-7/3, 2); **6.** (-2, 3); **7.** (2, -5); **8.** (-1, 4);
9. (1, -1/7); **10.** (6, 2); **11.** (-2, 3); **12.** (-2/3, 8);
13. Neither set of variables have opposite coefficients. To fix this, multiply the first equation by -3. Explanations will vary.

Page 74
1. Multiply first equation by 3.; **2.** Multiply second equation by 6.; **3.** Multiply second equation by 7.; **4.** Multiply second equation by -5.; **5.** (1, 1); **6.** (-2, 5); **7.** (1, 2); **8.** (-8, -9); **9.** (3, -3); **10.** (1, 1); **11.** (0, 4)

Page 75
1. a, one solution; **2.** c, one solution; **3.** d, infinitely many solutions (same line); **4.** b, no solution (parallel lines);
5. no solution
6. (1, -4), one solution
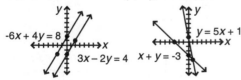
7. no solution
8. no solution

9. infinitely many solutions
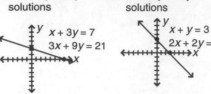
10. infinitely many solutions

11. infinitely many solutions
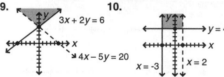
12. (4, 4) one solution
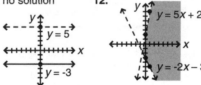

13. (3, 3) one solution
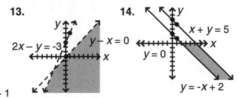

Page 76
1. solid, above; **2.** dashed, above; **3.** solid, below; **4.** dashed, above; **5.** solid, above; **6.** dashed, below;
7.
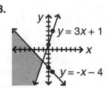
8.

9.
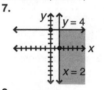
10.

11. no solution
12.

13.
14.

Page 77
1. Josh = 2 years, Cheryl = 8 years; **2.** 28, 22;
3. Joe's = $7.25, Jim's = $8.75; **4.** fries = $.75, hamburger = $1.00; **5.** quarters = 16, nickels = 24

Page 78
1. (-2, 1) is circled.; **2.** (-5, -5) is circled.;
3. no solution

4. (1/2, 5), one solution
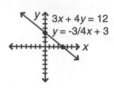

5. infinitely many solutions
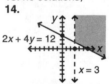
6. infinitely many solutions
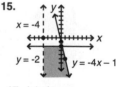

7. infinitely many solutions
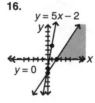
8. no solutions

9. (2, 5); **10.** (1, -1); **11.** (2, 0); **12.** (-4, -1);
13. mowing lawns = $5 per hour, walking dogs: $3 per hour

Page 79
1. yes; **2.–7.** Explanations will vary.
2. substitution, (-1, -2); **3.** adding, (8, 4);
4. substitution, (-4, -4); **5.** graphing, (3, -7);
6. substitution, (0, 1); **7.** multiplication and adding, (2, 4); **8.** no solution; **9.** one solution, (0, 2); **10.** one solution, (-1, 3); **11.** infinitely many solutions; **12.** infinitely many solutions; **13.** no solutions;
14.
15.
16.
17. John's age = 12 years, Mike's age = 36 years

Page 80
1. Add the exponents.; **2.** x: base, 3: exponent, x^3: power; **3.** Find the power of each factor and multiply.; **4.** $3x^3$; **5.** $36x^8y^5$; **6.** $-96x^3y^4z^{13}$;
7. $-4x^7$; **8.** $-128x^{11}y^{10}$; **9.** $-90x^{11}y^8$; **10.** x^4;
11. $-x^3y^3$; **12.** $15x^8$; **13.** $64x^{14}y^{14}z^{12}$

Page 81
1. 1; **2.** $1/x^8$; **3.** $x^2/3$; **4.** $1/x^3$; **5.** $1/x^{10}$; **6.** $x^4/5$;
7. $6x^2$; **8.** $6/x^3$; **9.** y^4/x^3; **10.** $8x^3$; **11.** $4/x^5$;
12. $4/x^4y^2$; **13.** $9/x^4$; **14.** 1/16; **15.** 1; **16.** 1;
17. -27; **18.** 1/1296; **19.** -8

Answer Key

Page 82
1. Subtract the exponents.; **2.** 125; **3.** 1; **4.** 729; **5.** 1/25; **6.** 27/8; **7.** 49; **8.** 1; **9.** 36; **10.** 16/25; **11.** 16/9; **12.** $27/x^3$; **13.** $1/x^2$; **14.** $-9x^4/y$; **15.** $1/x^2$; **16.** $2x^3y^5$; **17.** $7y^2/4x^{13}$; **18.** x^2; **19.** $14/y^2$; **20.** $2y^7/x^4$

Page 83
1. 208,000; **2.** 4,500; **3.** 0.0768; **4.** 0.000312; **5.** 0.00000625; **6.** 95,765; **7.** 6.8×10^7; **8.** 4.953×10^{-3}; **9.** 1.49×10^{12}; **10.** 9×10^9; **11.** 9.75×10^{-2}; **12.** 5.15×10^{-6}; **13.** 2.8×10^3; **14.** 1.5×10^4; **15.** 1.8×10^{-1}; **16.** 3.6×10^1 or 3.6×10; **17.** 7.2×10^{-7}; **18.** 3.5×10^6

Page 84
1.–6. Examples will vary. **1.** A monomial is an expression that can be a constant, a variable, or a product of a constant and one or more variables.; **2.** A trinomial is the sum of three monomials.; **3.** Standard form of a polynomial is the sum of terms in descending order, from largest degree to the smallest degree.; **4.** A binomial is the sum of two monomials.; **5.** The degree of a term is the power of the term.; **6.** A polynomial is a monomial or the sum of monomials.; **7.** $-x^3 - 4x^2 + 7x$, 3; **8.** $-x^5 - 4x^3 + 10x^2$, 5; **9.** $x^5 + x^4 + 3x^3 + 10$, 5; **10.** $9x^2 + 2x$, 2; **11.** $-2x^4 - 2x^3$, 4; **12.** $-9x^3 + 7x^2 - 7$, 3; **13.** $5x^7 + 2x^5 + 4x^4 - 6$, 7; **14.** $14x^3 - 4x^2 - 10x - 2$, 3

Page 85
1. Change the sign of each term in the second polynomial.; **2.** $4x - 12$; **3.** $-3x^2 - 9$; **4.** $14x + 4$; **5.** $-3x^4 - 7x^3 + 2x^2 + 2x$; **6.** $6x^2 - x + 5$; **7.** $2x^4 - 16x^3 + 5x$; **8.** $13x^2 + 7x + 5$; **9.** $-2x^2 - 3$; **10.** $-8x^2 + 7x - 3$; **11.** $2x - 16$; **12.** $6x^2 + 10x - 1$; **13.** $2x^2 - 4x - 2$

Page 86
1. $24x^2 - 18x$; **2.** $4x^3 - 24x^2 + 12x$; **3.** $12x^5 - 16x^4 + 8x^3$; **4.** $-5x^2 + 2x$; **5.** $15x^3 + 6x^2 + 10x$; **6.** $-5x^5 + 10x^4 - 5x^3$; **7.** $8x^2 + 16x$; **8.** $-7x^4 + x^3 - 4x^2$; **9.** $-10x^6 + 40x^5 - 30x^4$; **10.** $-x^2 + 19x + 1$; **11.** $6x^2 - 5x - 15$; **12.** $2x^2 + 21x$; **13.** $12x^2 + 12x + 6$; **14.** $20x^2 - 2x$; **15.** $-12x^3 + 4x^2 - 21x$; **16.** $-22x^2 + 43x - 69$; **17.** $8x^3 + x^2 - x$

Page 87
1. $x^2 + 2x - 35$; **2.** $x^2 - 10x + 25$; **3.** $54x^2 + 12x - 2$; **4.** $56x^2 - 113x + 56$; **5.** $x^2 + 5x + 6$; **6.** $x^2 - 49$; **7.** $-12x^2 - 41x - 35$; **8.** $3x^2 + 27x + 54$; **9.** $x^2 - 9x - 10$; **10.** $10x^2 - 7x - 12$; **11.** $-5x^2 + 16x - 12$; **12.** $-20x^2 - 12x + 32$; **13.** $6x^4 + 7x^2y - 20y^2$; **14.** $a^2x^2 + a^2y^2 + b^2x^2 + b^2y^2$; **15.** $32x^6 + 44x^5 - 6x^4$; **16.** $7x^3 - 2x^2 + 21x - 6$; **17.** $ax + ay + bx + by$; **18.** $x^4 - 3x^2 - 40$

Page 88
1. $x^2 - 16x + 64$; **2.** $4x^2 + 16x + 16$; **3.** $x^4 + 6x^2 + 9$; **4.** $9x^2 - 4$; **5.** $x^2 - 12x + 36$; **6.** $x^4 - 8x^2 + 16$; **7.** $x^2 - 49$; **8.** $49x^2 - y^2$; **9.** $16x^2 - 1$; **10.** $x^2 - 81$; **11.** $64x^2 - 32xy + 4y^2$; **12.** $4 - 36x^2$; **13.** $x = 10$; **14.** $x = 1$; **15.** $x = 4$; **16.** $x = -5$; **17.** $x = -5$; **18.** $x = -6$

Page 89
1. \$188.96; **2.** \$672.53; **3.** \$1929.70; **4.** \$1,455.02; **5.** \$1,574.64 (3 years at 8% less than 5 years at 5% (1,595.35), difference \$20.71

Page 90
1. $6x^6$; **2.** 16/25; **3.** x^3; **4.** $8y^6/x^2z^3$; **5.** $-24x^3y^5$; **6.** $x^{12}y^{24}z^{30}$; **7.** $-3/x^3y$; **8.** $2x^3y^5$; **9.** 314,500; **10.** 5.45×10^{-5}; **11.** $x - 5$, 1; **12.** $2x^5 - 8x^4 + 16x^3 - 4x + 2$, 5; **13.** $9x^2 - 13x - 4$, 2; **14.** $17x^3 - 8x^2 + 4x + 3$, 3; **15.** F–first terms, O–second terms, I–inner terms, L–last terms; Multiply each, then simplify.; **16.** $6x^4 - 14x^3 + 10x^2 - 4x$; **17.** $16x^2 - 16x + 4$; **18.** $3x^4 - 14x^2y - 24y^2$; **19.** 1,122.04

Page 91
1. multiplying — add exponents; dividing— subtract exponents; **2.** monomial—an expression that can be a constant, a variable, or a product of a constant and one or more variables; binomial—a sum of two monomials; trinomial—sum of three monomials; degree— actual power of the term with the highest degree; **3.** $-15y^7/x^3$; **4.** -24; **5.** $-2x^8/y^2z^4$; **6.** $9/8x^4y^{10}$; **7.** $8x^5$; **8.** $z^6/9x^4y^{10}$; **9.** 0.00000312; **10.** 4.619×10^{12}; **11.** $12x^4 - 8x^3 - 5x + 9$, 4; **12.** $8x^3 + 11x^2 - 5x - 11$, 3; **13.** $-15x^4 + 18x^3 - 6x^2$; **14.** $49x^2 - 28x + 4$; **15.** $-30x^2 - 16xy - 2y^2$; **16.** $x = -1/2$; **17.** \$629.71

Page 92
1. 9, -9; **2.** 0; **3.** 3/4, -3/4; **4.** 0.5, -0.5; **5.** 11, -11; **6.** 6/5, -6/5; **7.** undefined; **8.** 0.7, -0.7; **9.** -14; **10.** 0.2; **11.** -5/12; **12.** -2.5; **13.** 6.71; **14.** -11; **15.** 0.89; **16.** -7.07; **17.** 6; **18.** undefined; **19.** 9; **20.** 8; **21.** 8; **22.** 10

Page 93
Note: For 1–6, Multiply both sides by -1 if your *a* term is opposite the *a* term in the answer.
1. $x^2 + 3x - 5 = 0$, 3; **2.** $7x^2 - 5x - 10 = 0$, 7; **3.** $4x^2 - 6x - 15 = 0$, 2; **4.** $5x^2 - 4x - 6 = 0$; **5.** $-x^2 + 8x + 12 = 0$, -1; **6.** $-9x^2 + 5x + 8 = 0$, -9; **7.** +4; **8.** +13; **9.** ±10; **10.** ±10; **11.** ±8; **12.** ±11; **13.** ±7; **14.** ±9; **15.** ±6/5; **16.** ±4.06; **17.** ±3.46; **18.** ±8.12; **19.** ±2.24; **20.** ±2.83; **21.** ±8.94; **22.** ±2.65; **23.** ±3.87; **24.** ±3.16

Page 94
Note: For 1–6, if your *a* term is opposite the *a* below, multiply each side by -1.
1. $x^2 + 3x - 5 = 0$; $a = 1$, $b = 3$, $c = -5$; **2.** $-x^2 + 10 = 0$; $a = -1$, $b = 0$, $c = 10$; **3.** $-5x^2 + 12x - 10 = 0$; $a = -5$, $b = 12$, $c = -10$; **4.** $7x^2 - 5x + 12 = 0$; $a = 7$, $b = -5$, $c = 12$; **5.** $-4x^2 + 8x - 15 = 0$; $a = -4$, $b = 8$, $c = -15$; **6.** $2x^2 + 4x + 3 = 0$; $a = 2$, $b = 4$, $c = 3$; **7.** 4; **8.** 1; **9.** 44; **10.** 89; **11.** 109; **12.** 164; **13.** -1/3, -8; **14.** 10, 2; **15.** -2/5, -3/2; **16.** -4, -5; **17.** -3/4, -3/2; **18.** -3, -1/2

Page 95
1. $V = (0, 4)$, opens up, $x = 0$; **2.** $V = (-4, -13)$, opens up, $x = -4$; **3.** $V = (-2, 12)$, opens up, $x = -2$; **4.** $V = (3, -8)$, opens up, $x = 3$; **5.** $V = (-3, 14)$, opens down, $x = -3$; **6.** $V = (3, -25)$, opens up, $x = 3$; **7.** $V = (0, 2)$, opens down, $x = 0$; **8.** $V = (1, 2)$, opens down, $x = 1$; **9.** $V = (0, -2)$, opens down, $x = 0$;

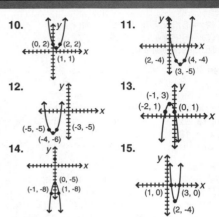

10. graph: (0, 2), (2, 2), (1, 1)
11. graph: (2, -4), (4, -4), (3, -5)
12. graph: (-5, -5), (-3, -5), (-4, -6)
13. graph: (-1, 3), (-2, 1), (0, 1)
14. graph: (0, -5), (-1, -8), (1, -8)
15. graph: (1, 0), (3, 0), (2, -4)

Page 96
1. 2^3; **2.** $2 \cdot 5$; **3.** $2 \cdot 3 \cdot 5^2$; **4.** $3^2 \cdot 5$; **5.** 3^2; **6.** $2^3 \cdot 5$; **7.** $2 \cdot 3^2 \cdot 5$; **8.** $2^2 \cdot 3 \cdot 5$; **9.** $2 \cdot 7$; **10.** $2^2 \cdot 7$; **11.** $2^3 \cdot 3^2 \cdot 5$; **12.** $2^3 \cdot 5^2$; **13.** 6; **14.** $8x^7$; **15.** x^2; **16.** 35; **17.** $4x^4$; **18.** $7x^2y^2$; **19.** $5a^2$; **20.** $3x^3$; **21.** $3x^2$

Page 97
1. 4; **2.** x^3; **3.** $2x$; **4.** x^2; **5.** 6; **6.** $3x^3$; **7.** $5x^2$; **8.** $5x$; **9.** $4x(x^2 - 6x + 8)$; **10.** $3x^2(3x^2 - 4x + 5)$; **11.** $6x(3x^2 + 8x - 4)$; **12.** $5x^2(2x^2 - 7x - 6)$; **13.** $x^4(x^2 + x + 1)$; **14.** $6x(2x^2 - 4x + 3)$; **15.** $4(x^2 - 2x + 3)$; **16.** $x^5(x^2 + x - 1)$; **17.** $4x(x^2 - 4x - 12)$; **18.** $5(5x^2 + 6x - 11)$; **19.** $11x^2(4x - 1)$; **20.** $4x^2(2x^4 + x^2 - 3)$; **21.** $3x(x^2 + 3x - 4)$; **22.** $7x(x - 3)$; **23.** $x(y^2 - y - 16)$; **24.** $3x^2(2x - 5)$; **25.** $9x(x^5 + 9x^2 - 3)$; **26.** $2(x^2y + 2x - 3y)$

Page 98
1. $(x + 10)(x - 10)$; **2.** $(8 + x)(8 - x)$; **3.** $(3 + x)(3 - x)$; **4.** $(1 + 9x)(1 - 9x)$; **5.** $(x + 7)(x - 7)$; **6.** $(x + 25)(x - 25)$; **7.** $(15x + 4)(15x - 4)$; **8.** $(3x + 5)(3x - 5)$; **9.** $(x + 5)^2$; **10.** $(x - 7)^2$; **11.** not a perfect square; **12.** not a perfect square; **13.** $(3x + 1)^2$; **14.** $(x - 2)^2$; **15.** $(11x + 8y)(11x - 8y)$; **16.** $(3x + 9y)^2$; **17.** $(5x + 15y)(5x - 15y)$; **18.** $(4x + 3y - 1)(4x - 3y + 1)$; **19.** $(7x + 5y)^2$; **20.** $(13x + 2y + 7)(-13x + 2y + 7)$; **21.** $(2x - 10y)^2$; **22.** $(6x + 7y)(6x - 7y)$

Page 99
1. 1, 2, 3, 6; +, +; **2.** 1, 5, 7, 35; +, -; **3.** 1, 2, 4, 7, 8, 14, 28, 56; -, -; **4.** 1, 2, 4, 5, 10, 20; -, -; **5.** 1, 2; +, +; **6.** 1, 3, 5, 9, 15, 45; +, +; **7.** 1, 2, 4, 7, 14, 28; +, -; **8.** 1, 2, 3, 5, 6, 10, 15, 30; +, -; **9.** 1, 2, 4; -, -; **10.** 1, 2, 4, 8, 16; +, +; **11.** 1, 2, 4, 5, 8, 10, 20, 40; +, -; **12.** 1, 2, 11, 22; +, -; **13.** $(x + 12)(x - 2)$; **14.** $(x - 20)(x + 2)$; **15.** $(x + 9)(x - 4)$; **16.** $(x + 17)(x - 1)$; **17.** $(x + 7)(x + 1)$; **18.** $(x - 5)(x + 4)$; **19.** $(x - 1)(x - 1) = (x - 1)^2$; **20.** $(x - 7)(x - 3)$; **21.** $(x - 5)(x - 2)$; **22.** $(x + 17)(x + 2)$; **23.** $(x - 8)(x + 6)$; **24.** $(x + 9)(x - 6)$; **25.** $(x - 8)(x + 2)$; **26.** $(x - 7)(x + 3)$; **27.** $(x + 8)(x + 7)$; **28.** $(x - 6)(x - 5)$

Page 100
1. 1, 3; 1, 2, 5, 10; **2.** 1, 2, 3, 6; 1, 11; **3.** 1, 2, 5, 10; 1, 5; **4.** 1, 2, 4, 7, 14, 28; 1, 3, 9; **5.** 1, 2, 4, 8; 1, 2, 3, 4, 6, 12; **6.** 1, 2, 3, 4, 6, 12; 1, 7; **7.** 1, 7; 1, 5, 7, 35; **8.** 1, 2, 4, 8, 16; 1, 2, 4; **9.** $(3x + 2)(x - 3)$; **10.** $(6x - 3)(2x + 5)$; **11.** $(9x + 3)(x - 1)$; **12.** $(2x + 3)(4x + 5)$; **13.** $(4x + 1)(2x - 6)$;

Answer Key

14. $(2x-6)(5x+4)$; **15.** $(5x-1)(x+2)$;
16. $(7x-5)(2x+7)$; **17.** $(3x+7)(2x-8)$;
18. Problems will vary.

Page 101
1. 3; **2.** 2; **3.** 4; **4.** 3; **5.** 1; **6.** 1; **7.** 4; **8.** 2;
9. $2(x+8)(x+2)$; **10.** $6(x+2y)(x-5y)$;
11. $2(5x+6y)(5x-6y)$; **12.** $x^3(6x^3+5x^2+7x+8)$; **13.** $3xy(x^2-3x+2y^2-5y)$; **14.** $2x(5x-4)(2x+1)$; **15.** $16(x+y)(x-y)$; **16.** $4(2x-1)^2$;
17. $x(x-6y)(x-y)$

Page 102
1. {-2, 3}; **2.** {-9, 0}; **3.** {-4, 0, 4}; **4.** {-7, 8};
5. {1, 10}; **6.** {-15, 0}; **7.** {-6, -4}; **8.** {-5, -2};
9. {-2, 0, 4}; **10.** {-7, -2, 0, 1}; **11.** $(x+8)(x-8)$; {8, -8}; **12.** $4x(x+2)(x-2)$; {-2, 0, 2}; **13.** $(2x+5)(2x-5)$; {-5/2, 5/2}; **14.** $x(3x+1)(x+1)$; {-1, -1/3, 0}; **15.** $x(x-14)$; {0, 14}; **16.** $4(x+4)^2$; {-4}; **17.** $(2x-1)(x+1)$: {-1, 1/2}; **18.** $(x+3)(x-1)$; {-3, 1}; **19.** $(x-5)^2$; {5}

Page 103
1. $3x-6=2x-12$; -6; **2.** $x^2=2x+8$; 4, -2;
3. $x^2+4x=12$; -6, 2; **4.** $2x^2=2x+4$; -1, 2;
5. $x(2x+6)=20$; -5, 2; **6.** $3x^2=16x-5$; 1/3, 5

Page 104
1. 5, -5; **2.** 9, -9; **3.** 7/6, -7/6; **4.** 10, -10; **5.** $a=1$; $b=-6$; $c=8$; 2, 4; **6.** $a=1$; $b=8$; $c=12$; -6, -2; **7.** $a=1$; $b=-2$; $c=-8$; 4, -2; **8.** $a=2$; $b=4$; $c=2$; -1; **9.** $a=3$; $b=6$; $c=-9$; -3, 1; **10.** $a=2$; $b=-4$; $c=-16$; -2, 4;

11.
12.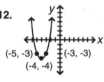

13.
14.

15.
16.

17. $5x^2$; **18.** 9; **19.** x^4; **20.** $3x$; **21.** $(x-3)(x-2)$; **22.** $(x-7)(x+4)$; **23.** $(3x+5y)^2$; **24.** $(3x-5)(x+2)$; **25.** $3x(x-4)(x+1)$; **26.** -14, 14; **27.** -5, 3

Page 105
1. $12=2^3 \cdot 3$, $48=2^4 \cdot 3$, $96=2^5 \cdot 3$; GCF = 12;
2. $18=2 \cdot 3^2$, $81=3^4$; $117=3^2 \cdot 13$; GCF = 9;
3. $30=2 \cdot 3 \cdot 5$, $60=2^2 \cdot 3 \cdot 5$, $120=2^3 \cdot 3 \cdot 5$, $150=2 \cdot 3 \cdot 5^2$; GCF = 30; **4.** $28=2^2 \cdot 7$, $49=7^2$, $84=2^2 \cdot 3 \cdot 7$; GCF = 7; **5.** -10, 10; **6.** -5/2, 5/2; **7.** -2/3, 2; **8.** -7, 7; **9.** 3, 4; **10.** -9, -3; **11.** opens up; See graph.; **12.** $3x^2(x^5-3x^4+2x^2-5)$; **13.** $12x(x-2y+3y^2)$; **14.** $9x^3y^2(2y^2-3xy-5x)$;

Page 106
1. -3; **2.** -3; **3.** -7, -1; **4.** -6, 3; **5.** 2; **6.** 4; **7.** -1, 6; **8.** 5; **9.** $2x/3$; **10.** $1/4x^3$; **11.** $1/x$; **12.** $x(x-2)$; **13.** -3/7; **14.** 2; **15.** $(x-6)/(x-2)$; **16.** $6/x$

Page 107
1. $-(6x+5)$; **2.** $-(x^2-36)$; **3.** $-1(x^2-y-52)$;
4. $2x^2-2x+11$; **5.** $-(x^2-10)$; **6.** $-(x^2-5x+7)$;
7. $-(x^2-9x+4)$; **8.** $-(9x+7)$; **9.** -1/5; **10.** $-1/(x+1)$; **11.** $-3x/(x-1)$; **12.** $-1/(x+6)$; **13.** $-(x-2)$;
14. $-1/(x+1)$; **15.** $-(x-1)$; **16.** $(-2x-3)/(x-4)$; **17.** -16; **18.** 5/3

Page 108
1. 40/99; **2.** $\frac{x^2-16x+64}{x+2}$; **3.** $\frac{-y^2}{x^2(x+3)}=\frac{-y^2}{x^3+3x^2}$;
4. -27/130; **5.** 1/2; **6.** 3; **7.** $\frac{7a^4}{20}$; **8.** $\frac{1}{-4x^2}$;
9. $\frac{-3x^3}{2y^5}$; **10.** $\frac{8y^6}{17x^8}$; **11.** 15/2; **12.** $\frac{-(x^2+6xy+5y^2)}{x^2-3xy+y^2}$;
13. $\frac{-2y^8}{3x^2}$; **14.** $\frac{2(x-6)}{x+5}=\frac{2x-12}{x+5}$

Page 109
1. 1/10; **2.** $\frac{1}{x+12}$; **3.** 4/3; **4.** $\frac{1}{x^2-7}$; **5.** $x-4$;
6. $\frac{x^2-5x+8}{3x^2}$; **7.** does not exist; **8.** $\frac{5x-12}{4x^2-3x+7}$;
9. 8; **10.** $-\frac{5}{8y^2}$; **11.** $3y$; **12.** $\frac{x^7}{y^8}$; **13.** $\frac{1}{5x^2-5x}$;
14. $\frac{x+1}{x+2}$; **15.** $-\frac{y^6}{z^7}$; **16.** $\frac{2x-16}{x+8}$; **17.** 3; **18.** $\frac{8}{x+3}$;
19. $\frac{2x-10}{5}$; **20.** $\frac{x^2-1}{x^2-x+6}$

Page 110
1. $17x/4$; **2.** $(x+1)/5$; **3.** 1/2; **4.** $13x^2/6$;
5. $(x-1)/x$; **6.** $6/x$; **7.** 1; **8.** $4/x$; **9.** $3/(x-3)$;
10. $(x+7)/x$; **11.** $5x/(x-6)$; **12.** $2x+2$;
13. $14x/s$; **14.** $48/x$

Page 111
1. 20; **2.** $24x^3$; **3.** $12xy$; **4.** $12x^3$; **5.** 21; **6.** $6x^6$;
7. $4x/5$; **8.** $\frac{6x+3}{8x}$; **9.** $\frac{-(2x^3-28x^2-45)}{20x^4}$; **10.** $x/4$;
11. $\frac{8x^2-3x+4}{4x^3}$; **12.** $\frac{15x+10}{12x}$; **13.** $\frac{5x+13}{4}$

Page 112
1. $(x-3)(x+2)$; **2.** $(x-1)(x+6)$; **3.** x; **4.** $x-3$;
5. $(2x+3)(x-4)$; **6.** x; **7.** x^2; **8.** $(x+2)$;
9. $\frac{6x-6}{x^2-3x}$; **10.** $\frac{21x+108}{x^2-36}$; **11.** $\frac{4x^2+14x-17}{4x-3}$;
12. $\frac{6x+35}{x+6}$; **13.** $\frac{x^2-6x+40}{x^2-16}$; **14.** $\frac{5x+6}{x^2-5x-14}$

Page 113
1. The denominator is 0.; **2.** Set denominator equal to 0 and find x values.; **3.** The least common denominator is the least factor that is a multiple of every factor in the denominators of every fraction in the given set of fractions.; **4.** Answers will vary.; **5.** 5, -2;
6. $\frac{3}{x^2}$; **7.** $\frac{x+4}{x-5}$; **8.** $x-8$; **9.** $-\frac{1}{x+1}$; **10.** $-\frac{3x^4-18x^3}{y^2}$;
11. $\frac{6x-12}{x-3}$; **12.** $\frac{4x^2}{y^4(x-4)}$; **13.** 2; **14.** $\frac{3}{x-3}$;
15. $\frac{9x+7}{24x^3}$; **16.** $\frac{6x^2+4x+3}{x^3}$; **17.** $x+2$

Page 114
1. A fraction whose numerator and denominator are polynomials; Examples will vary.; **2.** When values for the variables in the denominator make the denominator equal to ; **3.** 1) expression is written in descending order of exponents; 2) the first coefficient is positive; **4.** when adding or subtracting unlike terms; **5.** -4; **6.** 8; **7.** -9, 6; **8.** 0, 9; **9.** $\frac{12x^6y^8}{x^9}$;
10. $4/(x-4)$; **11.** $5x+20$; **12.** $(x+2)/(x-2)$;
13. 4; **14.** $(x-6)/(x+7)$; **15.** $\frac{-(5x-13)}{x-3}$; **16.** $\frac{6x-23}{6}$;
17. $\frac{21x^2+136x+108}{12x^2}$; **18.** $x-3$

Page 115
1. extremes = 4, 10; means = $3x$, 15;
2. extremes = x, 3; means = 4, 8; **3.** extremes = x, $x+2$; means = 2, 3; **4.** extremes = $x+4$, 7; means = 6, $x+7$; **5.** extremes = 5, n; means = 6, 45; **6.** extremes = 11, 121; means = x, 44; **7.** extremes = x, $x-5$; means = 3, 4;
8. extremes = 4, x; means = $x+8$, 3; **9.** 10;
10. 2; **11.** 7; **12.** 4, -4; **13.** 4; **14.** -4, 5; **15.** -9, 4;
16. 13, -13; **17.** A ratio is a comparison of two numbers by division. A proportion is two ratios set equal to each other.

Page 116
1. $12x$; **2.** $5x^3$; **3.** $6x^4$; **4.** $24x$; **5.** 3/2; **6.** 1/2; **7.** -3;
8. 0; **9.** 4; **10.** -5; **11.** 2, 5; **12.** -6; **13.** 8; **14.** 5

Page 117
1. $x=c/5$; **2.** $x=z-3y$; **3.** $x=4y$; **4.** $x=\frac{z}{y-w}$;
5. $x=y+z$; **6.** $x=-z/y$; **7.** $x=\frac{5y+2bc+2}{k}$; **8.** $x=\frac{a-c}{b}$; **9.** $\ell=\frac{P-2w}{2}$, $\ell=24$ in.; **10.** Answers will vary.

Page 118
1. 80°, 100°; **2.** 600 miles; **3.** 1,200 in.²; **4.** 12 eggs; **5.** 36°, 54°; **6.** 66 in.

Page 119
1. 1/3 of the document; $n/6$ of the document;
2. 3/4; **3.** 6 6/13 hours; **4.** 4 4/9 hours; **5.** 11 1/4 hours; **6.** 58 2/3 hours

Page 120
1. a comparison of two numbers by division; Example will vary; **2.** two ratios set equal to each other; Example will vary.; **3.** Example and explanation will vary.; **4.** $30x^3$; **5.** extremes = $x+2$, x^2; means = 9, x; **6.** 15; **7.** 6; **8.** -24; **9.** -9; **10.** -4, -1; **11.** -5; **12.** -4; **13.** -8/3; **14.** 6;
15. $w=\frac{P-2\ell}{2}$, $w=23$ in.; **16.** 900 g of flour; **17.** 11 1/4 hours; **18.–19.** Examples will vary.

Page 121
1. A ratio is a comparison of two numbers by division. A proportion is two ratios equal to each other. Examples will vary.; **2.** extremes: $4x$, 11; means = 7, 6; **3.** 1) Multiply each side of the equation by the LCM of the fractions in the equation. 2) Simplify each term in the equation. 3) Solve for x.; **4.** an equation that contains more than one letter as a variable;
5. x^3-9x; **6.** 20; **7.** 8; **8.** 0, 6; **9.** 7; **10.** -2. 1;
11. 31; **12.** 6,000 people; **13.** sister = 10 1/2 hours; Toby = 21 hours; **14.** $x=\frac{z}{a+b}$;
$b=\frac{z-ax}{x}$; **15.** 104 m²; **16.** 40°, 140°